Nature's Keeper

John Ripley Forbes
and the Children's Nature Movement

Gary Ferguson

Softcover:
ISBN 10: 1-59152-085-1
ISBN 13: 978-1-59152-085-6

Hardcover:
ISBN 10: 1-59152-086 -X
ISBN 13: 978-1-59152-086-3

Published by John Ripley Forbes Big Trees Forest Preserve, Inc.

Cover photo: Sergeant John Ripley Forbes, launching a nature
museum in Geneva County, Alabama in 1943.

For more information, write:
Gary Ferguson, PO Box 1490, Red Lodge, MT 59068.

You may order extra copies of this book by calling
Farcountry Press toll free at (800) 821-3874.

s♦eetgrassbooks
a division of Farcountry Press

Produced by Sweetgrass Books, PO Box 5630, Helena, MT 59604;
(800) 821-3874; www.sweetgrassbooks.com.

The views expressed by the author/publisher in this book do
not necessarily represent the views of, nor should be attributed to,
Sweetgrass Books. Sweetgrass Books is not responsible for
the content of the author/publisher's work.

Printed in the United States.

16   15   14   13   12   1   2   3   4   5   6   7

Acknowledgments

THIS BOOK COULD NOT HAVE BEEN WRITTEN without the kind help of dozens of people who across the decades lived and worked with John Ripley Forbes; their memories and insights have been invaluable. Special thanks to Charles S. Roberts, President of the Big Trees Forest Preserve, who both recognized the positive influence of John's work with the children's nature movement, and at the same time, committed himself to helping pass it on to future generations. My sincere appreciation goes as well to the city of Sandy Springs, Georgia, which provided important financial support for the research of this publication.

Thanks to archivist Joan Clemens for her excellent work sorting and categorizing John's papers, letters and photographs. And to the wonderful research staff of the Hawthorne-Longfellow Library at Bowdoin College. Finally, my enduring gratitude to the Forbes family—John's wife Margaret, as well as their children Ripley and Anne—without whom this glimpse of a truly inspired life might never have happened.

Contents

Introduction

STAMFORD, CONNECTICUT, 1928. As in most major cities across southern New England, bedlam arrives here Monday through Saturday evenings at five o'clock sharp. First comes the shrill, ragged wailing of factory whistles, followed by thousands of workers pouring out of brick buildings into parking lots and onto the streets and sidewalks of the business district. Most are at the end of ten-hour shifts making pin-tumbler locks at the Yale and Towne factory. Or assembling typewriters for Blickensderfer. Stamping out razor blades and ice cream scoops for Excelsior Hardware. Constructing postage meters for Pitney Bowes.

Walking among the groups of chattering laborers as they make their way back to the neighborhoods, it would be easy to lose count of the languages being spoken: Polish and German, Italian, Greek, Croatian, and more. Some street corners hold the smooth drawl of southern black men, fresh in from Georgia and Mississippi to work the foundries and wire factories. Elsewhere is the thick brogue of the

Irish—part of the soundscape here since the great potato famine sent thousands westbound across the Atlantic some seventy-five years earlier.

Yet even in these hectic, fast-moving days—days of jazz on the radio and Charles Lindbergh over the Atlantic—New Englanders are showing an astonishing fondness for nature. Giggling children point at robins shaking themselves free of the tree canopies, flying off to the lawns at Town Hall to pluck worms for their hungry offspring. Six blocks away, picnickers watch red knots and plovers and rafts of geese working the shorelines and bays of Long Island Sound, gobbling calories before resuming their journeys north. Since the decline of farming, vast runs of forest have sprouted around the city; a web of new walking trails meanders through the young maple and beech and chestnut trees crowding the old stone walls along the Mianus River and, to the northwest, near Chestnut Hill, among dark, sweet-smelling runs of hemlock. "This is a landscape in which the natural and built environments are balanced on a human scale," New England historian Richard Ewald would later write. It was that precious balance, he claimed, that formed "the nature of our community character."

While Ewald's remarks resonated with many, they seem especially appropriate for one Stamford citizen in particular: a gangly, fifteen-year-old preacher's son by the name of John Ripley Forbes. At the end of most school days, Forbes can be found making a beeline out of the classroom, scurrying for his home at the rectory of St. Andrew's Episcopalian Church on Washington Street. Once inside the imposing granite building, he climbs the stairs to the third floor, pushes open the door to a stuffy attic, switches on the light. There he stands for a time with hands in pockets, a look of intense concentration on his face. On this particular day he's carefully considering an altogether fabulous new acquisition: a possum, dead as a post, victim of a speeding car two days earlier, tossed into a sack by a couple of thoughtful chums who knew well how much he'd cherish the carcass.

Skinned and mounted, it will be a perfect addition to the sprawling run of natural curiosities Forbes has assembled beneath the slanted ceilings: bird mounts and eggs, snake skins and arrowheads and rock samples, butterflies and insects and terrariums and fish bowls. And outside in the yard, live creatures, most held just long enough for him to study: rabbits and squirrels, mice, injured birds. And snakes. Always snakes. Hard-to-manage serpents that are forever escaping confinement and making their way inside the house to the kitchen, or to the toilet, and at least once, slithering among the boxy wooden pews of the sanctuary minutes before the start of his father's Sunday service.

On this day, though, moving in for a closer look, Forbes wrinkles his nose. After forty-eight hours in a hot attic, the prized possum is starting to decay. But as John pulls his taxidermy supplies from the drawer in the corner of the room—knife and salt, cornmeal and forceps—the family dog, a harebrained spaniel named Pete, picks up the scent of ripening flesh and with an eager nose pushes open the attic door. Before the young naturalist knows what's happening, Pete snatches the rotting carcass and carries it down the oak stair treads into the living room, proudly dropping it at the feet of Mrs. Forbes.

If only she'd been alone. But not today. Today she's surrounded by a group of freshly scrubbed, carefully perfumed church ladies in modest, loose-fitting cotton dresses—women who up until this very minute had been in high spirits, floating in the refined pleasures of afternoon tea with the reverend's wife. On spotting the carcass, one woman panics. Then another. Writing about the incident later, Forbes sums up the scene with the kind of matter-of-fact detachment befitting a man of science: "All the ladies," he remarks coolly, "arose in wild disorder." Out beyond the screen door, beyond the women's gasps and screams, robins are chirping. A gray squirrel chatters loudly from a maple tree at a passing group of factory men. In the backyard snakes are testing their cages, poking their noses into the corners and cracks, finally pausing, uncoiling into the warm rays of the sun.

When John Ripley Forbes took his first walks through the woods near Boston as a little boy with his minister father, looking for those places where God and science met among the chipmunks and the oak trees and the bird nests, he was at the tail end of a movement as energetic as any in history—a force, as the popular *Century Magazine* put it, "which has no counterpart anywhere in the world." A time when naturalists like John Burroughs and Ernest Thompson Seton were as popular as today's rock stars. When, for nearly two decades, the *Boy Scouts Handbook* was outselling every book in the country except the Bible. In the same month as John's birth, August 1913, a part-time artist named Joe Knowles stripped down to something akin to a G-string, running off into the woods of western Maine to live as a wild man for two months. It was a noble act, Knowles said, meant to prove that Americans "still had sap in their veins." He emerged eight weeks later a national hero. The book about his adventures, *Alone in the Wilderness*, became a bestseller. He went on to travel vaudeville for two and a half years with top billing.

Yet for all this celebration of the natural world, Forbes would also be shaped by the fact that this same era—stretching from roughly the mid-1890s until the Great Depression—was marked by growing anguish that, in many places, the land was being slowly but surely overwhelmed by urbanization. Despite promises in the middle 1800s that the industrial revolution would all but end human suffering, by 1900 thousands of former farm dwellers were spending long days in sweltering factories, most pocketing wages worth less in terms of spending power than a decade earlier. One of every five children worked in sweatshops. Respiratory illness was skyrocketing, leading hundreds of doctors to recommend their patients pick up stakes and move to healthier climates in the interior West. Pundits of the late nineteenth century were worried: if nature had been such a big part of who we were as a people—indeed, if it had in fact been the fundamental ingredient of American identity—then who would we be when nature was gone?

Much of the audience for Forbes' work as an outdoor educator (including the wealthy benefactors whose money he regularly liberated for the cause) were greatly concerned that serious harm would befall children cut off from the outdoors. Even now, one of the most talked about nature books of the past decade has been Richard Louv's 2005 title, *Last Child in the Woods: Saving Our Children from Nature Deficit Disorder*. What Louv points to, bolstered by an impressive array of modern scientific research, differs little from what many educators knew in more general terms a century ago. The modern claim that time spent in nature tends to sharpen concentration, for example—a fact that's given rise to a new flush of interest in using the outdoors as a therapeutic milieu for treating attention deficit disorder—was understood a half century before ADD was even named. Likewise, educators in the early twentieth century routinely pointed out the power of nature to heal emotional trauma as well as to foster higher levels of creativity in young children.

Arguably, Forbes would accomplish as much in service of these concerns as any person in history—helping to launch some 200 nature centers and preserves from coast to coast and, in his later years, saving dozens of key parcels of land from hungry developers. If today in America there's a fresh willingness to return to such values, to employ outdoor settings—including urban gardens—for the benefit of our children, it's somehow comforting to know we're rekindling passions for the outdoors long a part of our national heritage.

Walk into any of the hundreds of outdoor centers John Ripley Forbes helped inspire, and you'll find children overflowing with questions: *Why do the baby deer have spots? Why does that bird wear bright colors, while the one over there is plain?* By age fifteen or sixteen, those questions become more sophisticated: *Why is this corner of the forest sick and dying? Is it prolonged drought, weakening the trees and making them susceptible to beetles? Could it be acid rain? If so, where's the pollution coming from? Given that trees filter air pollution, that they're important for sequestering excess carbon dioxide in the atmosphere, what are the possible effects of losing the forest? Are there solutions to the problem? How much will they cost? How long do we have?*

Forbes' outdoor classrooms offered much more than simply learning the names of plants and animals. Studying nature, he believed, would on one hand ignite in children a sense of wonder, an appreciation for beauty. But he also knew such settings as places to train the mind to think in terms of connections—connections that may well hold answers to issues ranging from global warming to safe food supplies, from flood control to the rise of pollution-related disease. Out of the millions of hours American boys and girls have spent in Forbes-inspired nature centers across the country, to this day many walk out of the woods having gained more expansive ways of thinking about the world.

Time Magazine was right to call Forbes the "Johnny Appleseed" of America's nature centers. Across more than seven decades he kept notions of birds and rivers and woodlands simmering in people's hearts and minds. And if such images are bound to grow faint now and then, nearly swallowed up by our busy, technology-laden lives, then at least in much of the country there is not far away one of John's walking trails, a nature center, maybe a children's museum— each and every pathway, every slice of forest, keeping the promise of nature from ever drifting out of reach. ✎

Sergeant John Ripley Forbes, launching a nature museum in Geneva County, Alabama in 1943.

Chapter One

THE HOME WOODS

MANY OF THE IDEAS BEHIND JOHN'S WORK—the work of providing doorways into nature for America's children—rested in the outdoor movements of the late nineteenth century, several of which had taken root in his home region of New England. The famous "fresh air camps" movement of the 1880s brought a flurry of programs to the lakes and woodlands near urban areas in the Northeast, part of an attempt to give poor, inner-city children—many of whom were recently arrived immigrants—a much-needed chance to visit the outdoors. A single piece of that effort—the Trail Blazer Camps, established in 1887 by the publisher of *Life* magazine—would over thirty years serve more than 40,000 children. Common wisdom of the time said that making nature available to disadvantaged kids would improve everything from physical health to personal motivation. Educators, social theorists, and politicians like Teddy Roosevelt argued that juvenile delinquency would be less of a problem if we simply cultivated in children a positive relationship to nature.

At the other end of the socioeconomic spectrum were places like Camp Chocorua, established in 1881 on New Hampshire's Big Squam Lake by Ernest Balch, to counter what Balch saw as the dismal summer life of wealthy boys from New York and Boston, most of whom were relegated to idle nonsense at upscale resorts. The first principle of such an endeavor, Balch wrote, was that "there should be no servants in the camp," that the work "must all be done by the boys and faculty." He claimed campers should be given the chance to build confidence through systematic instruction in swimming, diving, boat work, canoeing, and sailing—or, as Balch put it, through "mastering the lake."

Some people thought Balch's ideas absurd. But in a stroke of good fortune, his program caught the attention of beloved Civil War hero and renowned educator General Samuel Chapman Armstrong. Intrigued by Balch's ideas, Armstrong decided to spend two weeks living at Chocorua, studying the program's effects. At the end of the session, he found himself surrounded by happy, enthusiastic kids, many of whom seemed far more confident and creative than at the start, and sporting a newfound willingness to be part of a team. Armstrong wasted little time heaping praise for Camp Chocorua in dozens of newspapers and magazines across the country. Almost overnight, enthusiasm increased widely among the wealthy to send their kids to summer camp.

While New England was busy sprouting summer camps, many of the adults in Forbes' future hometown of Stamford, Connecticut, were signing up for the Agassiz Association, founded in honor of internationally famous biologist Louis Agassiz. "Whether you are four or eighty-four," the group advised its members, "be an original investigator. See things for yourself. Look into the thing, not into what has been written about the thing—what you find, not what someone tells you to find." A relationship to the natural world, they suggested, "was never more needed than in this age of artificiality, of the nervous stress and strain of the modern struggle for existence, of the tension of high keyed life, of intense competition, of financial fluctuations and of varying prosperity and adversity." Nature study, Louis Agassiz had argued, fostered both creative perspective and rigorous thought—essential qualities in good times or bad. In due time John Ripley Forbes would be carrying such ideas in his pockets like precious seeds, planting them across the twentieth century from coast to coast.

Such boundless enthusiasm for nature would have been unthinkable to that disgruntled group of Puritans who first parted company with their fellow colonists in nearby Wethersfield in 1641, heading south to set up homes on what at the time were Algonquin lands, on the banks of the Rippowam River near today's Stamford. The same unkempt lands that were by the mid-1800s being described as a source of spiritual health—the forest as a place people go to glimpse the genius of the Creator—had in the 1600s been thought by the Puritans to be hiding places for the devil. The Puritans would have been especially appalled that by the time John Forbes was falling in love with the woods, many of his neighbors—rather than shuffling back inside a dark sanctuary for another round of fervent prayer—were thinking it just fine to cart their souls off for a Sunday afternoon picnic at Cove Pond, using the outdoors as a means not to escape spiritual concerns but to more fully address them. As the hugely popular New England naturalist John Burroughs put it, "If we do not go to church as often as our forefathers, then we go to the woods much more."

In 1922 John Ripley Forbes' father, Reverend Kenneth Forbes, bought a small summer cottage for his family on New Hampshire's Lake Winnipesaukee. Outdoor Sunday church services, including so-called "floating vespers" like this one off Jolly Island, had long been a favorite of summer residents.

Even many preachers were by this point friendly to such notions—including John's father, Kenneth Forbes. By the time John entered grade school, and as automobile travel became ever more common, families across southern New England were pledging allegiance to nature in a brand-new way, spending as much of their summers as possible at rustic lake cottages, or "camps," in Maine, Vermont, and New Hampshire. Outdoor church services were a staple of such adventures, hosted by preachers prone to linking the kindness of the Creator to the beauty of creation.

At New Hampshire's Lake Winnipesaukee—where in 1922 the Forbes family joined the cottage crowd—weekly services were held on both Jolly and Birch Islands, as well as out on the water by means of "floating vespers." As far back as 1897, a charismatic parson by the name of Captain Luce had dropped anchor in the lee of Birch Island, preaching evening services to crowds gathered in a loose circle of rowboats. At the close of service the bobbing congregation sang the sun down to a run of old Christian hymns. "Someone would offer a brief prayer at the end," wrote one historian, "and as the sun sank below the horizon the boats would quietly drift away singing 'God be with you till we meet again.'" Families quietly rowed away, guided toward their homes by kerosene lanterns left burning on the shore.

The Forbes' modest cottage was tucked into the woods of eighteen-acre Birch Island. By the time of their arrival, the Methodists were already well established, offering services every Sunday afternoon in an open-air grove known as the "Birch Island Cathedral." But Kenneth Forbes, showing the kind of single-mindedness that one day would also describe his son John, had his own ideas of a proper liturgy. In a matter of weeks he developed an entirely different service, giving his own nod to God at a small birch altar erected directly behind the family cottage. From this rustic podium he celebrated the miracles of the natural world, reminding his congregation that God had not so much given all this to humans but had instead entrusted it to their care. At seven o'clock every Sunday morning, John and his two brothers, fully dressed in vestments, took up the duties of acolytes, coming and going under the branches of the birch and the hemlocks.

It's likely young John would have fallen in love with nature no matter where he landed—be it a wild preserve or an urban woodlot. And yet, Winnipesaukee (roughly translated as "beautiful water of the high place") took an unflinching hold on him, stoking a passion for the mysteries of the woods and waterways that would last the rest of his life. If Kenneth Forbes was determined to feed and water Christian faith in the Lakes Region of New Hampshire, John would, by his teen years, be known as the guy who spread the gospel of the outdoors—leading outings and founding a tiny nature center. Ultimately, in the 1970s he would launch one of the most significant regional preservation movements of the latter twentieth century.

John's own writings, which he began around age fourteen, read like the narrative of a long and fabulous field trip: A morning spent tracking a distant hammering in the forest, at trail's end laying eyes for the first time on a pileated woodpecker. Carefully approaching a black-throated green warbler feasting on a dragonfly, in the end getting close enough to stroke the bird's head. Hearing the haunting laugh of loons, and on calm evenings the song of whippoorwills drifting across the water from Bear Island. One day while out exploring, he ran across a small willow, two of its branches drooping under the weight of thousands of two-inch-long black spiny caterpillars—each one, he noted, sporting eight dots along the middle of its back. Carefully plucking several dozen of the creatures, John carried them home, where, consulting his field guides, he determined them to be larvae of the mourning cloak butterfly. For two full days he faithfully fed the caterpillars, at which point they stopped eating.

"They attached themselves to the wire covering of the box," he writes, "hanging suspended by their posterior prolegs fastened into a carpet of silk with the body curved upward." Two weeks later, thirty of the original forty caterpillars emerged as mourning cloaks. Forbes was especially interested in how, when he picked up one of the butterflies, it would close its wings, fold its feet, and play dead. Unable to rouse it by passing it back and forth from hand to hand, he let it drop softly to the ground, where he noted in great detail the slow, cautious unfolding of the creature, followed by sudden flight.

Day after day, sometimes by boat and other times by foot, he followed mink and brown bats, skunks and moles and white-footed mice, milk and ribbon and ring-neck and banded water snakes. John's interest in birds was especially strong, and his list of sightings swelled in no time to an impressive seventy-two species. If his early encounters were more or less random, over time his observations

Twelve year-old John Ripley Forbes, returning to the family cottage on Birch Island after a successful afternoon of fishing on Lake Winnipesaukee, in east-central New Hampshire. The joy John felt during summers at the Lake took firm hold, stoking in him a passion for the woods and waterways of New England that would last the rest of his life.

taught him to anticipate a surprising range of events. By age fourteen he had a strong sense of the creatures themselves. By fifteen he understood a great deal about the context of their behavior— the patterns and relationships that bound them to the larger world. He took every opportunity to explain his discoveries—not just at Winnipesaukee but to anyone who cared to climb the stairs to his attic museum in Stamford.

Forbes describes his early years in school as "turbulent," confessing to having "little interest in vital studies. I would spend long hours playing with snakes, birds, bugs and the like, but it required force of parents and teachers to get me to spend any time on arithmetic, spelling, or other practical and necessary studies." Perhaps not surprisingly, as he grew older he flirted with the fine art of playing hooky, at one point spreading his older brother's talcum powder on his face to achieve just the right pale, sickly look for the classroom. The ruse worked beautifully. On being sent home, he headed straight for a certain fish market where he sometimes made money as a delivery boy, often working to pay for tickets to big screen crime dramas and other "forbidden neighborhood movies."

Although John claimed many of his neighbors "could almost see halos above our heads," smiling at the sight of his brothers and him following their mother from church at the end of Sunday services, he also admitted to having his share of "wholesome boyhood activities of a devilish nature." Clandestine meetings were held, often to hatch plans for various practical jokes, as part of the top secret Red Caps Club, which for a time met in the trap-doored room of the sixty-foot church tower. Then there was the day the poor drunk man stumbled up to the church and, after John told him about his "pets," mumbled that yes indeed, he'd very much like to meet them, only to minutes later be horrified when John pulled from a large box a snake several feet long. "He threw himself prostrate on the ground in the most approved 'Allah-be-praised' manner. His prayerful mutterings, though incoherent, were very earnest."

Among John's most memorable shenanigans was the evening he and a pal named Luis went to the church for a Boy Scout meeting, only to discover it had been rescheduled. As it happened, other people were meeting at the church that night, including a certain club filled with young girls. Claiming inspiration from the full moon, he and Luis went to an unused room upstairs and set about making a ghost out of choir vestments. They rigged the ghost with an elaborate rope-and-string contraption so it could be spun about in the rafters, then turned off the lights. "Up the long flight [of stairs] labored a small heavyset boy, loaded down with some fifteen hymn books piled up to his chin. As he reached the top stair he spied the ghost, which rose from its perch and floated gently toward him. Choir books flew in all directions and the terrified boy fell. Down the long staircase he tumbled, screaming for his mother at the top of his lungs." The way the boy yelled, John writes, bringing everyone at the church running from all directions, "one would have thought the skin would peel from his throat." The happy, if somewhat anxious pranksters ripped down the rope and threw the ghost into a nearby closet, then leapt out an open window onto the roof, slid down a drainpipe, and disappeared into the night.

Beyond endless hours spent exploring fields and woodlots, lakes and streams, John also had the benefit of regular visits to three of the most original, energetic museums in the nation: the Boston Children's Museum, the Brooklyn Children's Museum, and the American Museum of Natural History. Many an afternoon he spent wandering past glass cases filled with arrowheads and bird mounts, running eager fingers across geodes and spear points and animal skins, and on most days, hitting up the museum staff for answers to an endless string of questions.

At fifteen he met celebrated zoologist and conservationist William T. Hornaday, beginning a friendship that would last the remainder of the older man's life. At the time, Hornaday was a household name

No one had a more lasting impact on John Ripley Forbes than his first mentor, the great zoologist William Hornaday, former director of the Bronx Zoo. After Hornaday's death in the spring of 1937, John quickly established a foundation in his honor; in the years that followed the foundation helped create dozens of children's nature museums and outdoor centers across the country.

throughout the United States, in large part for his dogged efforts to save the last of a once-grand bison population in the American West, which by the late nineteenth century had been nearly slaughtered out of existence. He also had a hand in creating two of the best, and in many ways "kindest," zoos of his day, designed largely to give scientific voice to the importance of preservation.

A half century earlier, working as a taxidermist in Sarasota Springs, New York, Hornaday had astonished the scientific world by creating a display of orangutan mounts in a jungle setting so real you could almost smell the figs and hear the whistling thrush. Based in part on that work, he was invited to join the team at the Smithsonian Museum, where he was initially put in charge of caring for the museum's live animals—animals whose major purpose was to serve taxidermists, who used them as models for rendering their mounts as natural looking as possible.

In a move that forty years later could have easily been engineered by Forbes, Hornaday concocted a tiny live animal exhibit on the grounds of the Smithsonian, behind the Castle building. Overnight, excited crowds were elbowing one another to glimpse the bear and the badgers, the eagle and the bison, some of which Hornaday had gathered during collecting expeditions in the American West. Encouraged by the public response, Hornaday spent the next five years plotting and arm twisting, finally convincing Congress in 1889 to approve the establishment of what would become the National Zoo—arguing that the facility could, among other things, be used to propagate disappearing wildlife. With help from Frederic Law Olmsted, Hornaday pushed for the zoo to not be merely a collection of isolated animals in spare confinement, as was the norm at the time, but to create spaces that would closely resemble the animals' natural habitats. "If an animal will not live happily in captivity," argued Hornaday, "do not keep it in captivity."

Unfortunately, such ideas were less to the liking of Smithsonian secretary Samuel Langley. The two men argued loud and often over the matter, and in the end Hornaday decided to leave the Smithsonian altogether. Given his golden reputation, it took little time before the New York Zoological Society approached him, asking if he'd consider directing an existing zoo in the middle of New York City. And a bleak, impoverished zoo it was, made up of little more than a fenced-in field with a dozen or so animals, many sick and lethargic. From that humble beginning Hornaday went on to create the legendary Bronx Zoo, where he would remain for the next thirty years.

Throughout his life the zoologist had shown enormous fondness for children, writing them long, patient letters of advice, now and then gently chiding those who had leveled some offense against wildlife. Thus it was a fine twist of fortune that finally landed him, freshly retired, at a house on North Street in Stamford, just blocks from John Ripley Forbes and his attic full of bird eggs and snakes and dead possum. One day while out on a hike with the Boy Scouts, fifteen-year-old Forbes stumbled on a small frog in the woods with a strange glow in its stomach. Clearly stumped, John's mother suggested he run it by the old zoologist on North Street. That afternoon, mother and son knocked on Hornaday's door and right away were welcomed inside. Sitting in the study, the seventy-three-year-old and the fifteen-year-old began a lengthy discussion, eventually concluding that the frog's stomach was glowing because not long before it had swallowed a firefly.

Upon leaving, John's mother invited Hornaday to see the natural history collection her son had laid out in the attic of the rectory. Eager as ever to encourage such passions in young people, Hornaday walked the three blocks to St. Andrew's Episcopalian Church, then made the long, slow climb up three flights of stairs to the top of the rectory. Expecting to find at best a glorified science fair project, the old scientist was speechless. "I came to see a boy's collection," Hornaday told John's mother, "but instead I have seen a scientific museum. Your son is a born curator." Soon afterward, Hornaday talked to friends at the Bruce Museum in nearby Greenwich, convincing them to turn over a portion of their basement to young John, who wasted no time enlarging his collections.

Years later Hornaday expressed the hope that John Forbes would "render good service to people who are slipping away from the old standards of general natural history"—that he would "develop into an old-fashioned, all-around zoologist." What Hornaday wanted in the next generation of scientists wasn't just academic excellence but a commitment to advocacy—a willingness to fight to protect the living objects they studied. By the time Hornaday ran across young Forbes, he'd grown weary of timid scientists, men too cautious to pressure politicians into making sound conservation choices. The role of the scientist, he complained, was growing ever smaller and safer, and consequently, much less useful to the nation. To Hornaday, what had once been pursuit of knowledge driven by respect for the resource was becoming little more than an exercise in clinical thinking. He often lamented how many of his colleagues were ignoring issues of extinction, "never spending a dollar or lifting an active finger on the firing line in defense of wild life." Science, in other words, was losing its heart. And that, Hornaday predicted, would among other things have terrible consequences for America's children.

Building on the massively popular "Bird Day"—first established in 1894, and in many ways strikingly similar to our current Earth Day—Hornaday implored teachers across the country to impart to students "the duty of every good citizen to take an active, aggressive part in preventing the destruction of wild life," claiming that "every boy and girl over twelve years of age can do something in this cause." He routinely expressed concerns about how science was being taught to young children. When it came to teaching kids, he argued, what was needed was not dispassionate lessons but living, breathing inquiry. During his tenure at the Bronx Zoo, he'd been adamant that zoology should never be taught "without adequately introducing the animals themselves." The pupil should learn first about the birds of use and beauty, he explained, as well as "the big animals that are being so rapidly exterminated—the injurious rodents, the rattlesnakes and moccasins, the festive alligator, the turtles." He decried the practice of asking children early on to "write twelve paragraphs on the mouth parts of a crayfish," saying such clumsy requests would likely rob them of the pleasure that could come from "a good general knowledge of the most interesting animal species."

Forbes was taking notes. What intrigue could science hold for children, he would argue years later, if it was detached from the human delights of beauty and curiosity? How could we expect to unleash the steps necessary for a child to learn—specifically, hands-on experience and patient reflection—without saving the very natural areas where such qualities were most readily experienced? In a sense both he and Hornaday were philosophically in legion with another famous New Englander, world-renowned educational reformer John Dewey, who would arguably have as much influence on public schools as anyone in the nation's history. Dewey cared less about the mastery of facts (that peculiar obsession that Hornaday fretted was killing the soul of science) than about teaching children how to think. Understanding something in a way that totally isolated it from human experience, said Dewey, was to have scant knowledge of it at all.

As John's career unfolded, he planted such notions in countless nooks and crannies of American culture. As World War II raged on, he would refer to nature centers in terms similar to how Dewey described the role of public schools: as instruments of societal repair. People used to seeing things from a variety of angles and influences, Forbes argued—exactly what nature study trained a person's mind to do—not only would possess skills for solving tough societal problems but would be more likely to accurately assess the hyperbole of politicians and corporate tycoons. Against the background of a world at war, in a 1942 essay about nature museums for the *National Humane Review*, Forbes talked of children having in nature "the chance to watch the butterfly as it slowly emerges from its chrysalis, see tadpoles change into frogs, watch eggs hatch into birds or into snakes." For children who experienced such feelings of connection, said John, "there is every reason to believe there is being instilled sympathy and understanding that may well affect their attitudes toward all living creatures." In the face of these tumultuous times, he suggested, "let us direct [children's] minds to channels that will keep foremost in their thoughts kindness, justice, understanding, love."

In other words, to not provide children with encounters in nature was to deny them far more than just beauty and fresh air. Nature's great stewpot of wonders—her complex relationships, her vitality, and certainly her ability to prompt compassion—offered nothing less than the chance for children to walk strong in the world.

In concert with this emerging eagerness to refresh the links between culture and nature, natural history museums would become marks of distinction. The city of Stamford had been angling for one since 1845, when the local Lyceum tried and failed to build a showcase regional nature center. Sixty-six years later, in 1911, Dr. Edward F. Bigelow of the Agassiz Association pleaded strongly for such a facility in his publication *The Guide to Nature*. He had good momentum going, too, though in the end he jumped ship for the town of Greenwich, where he established the much-celebrated Bruce Museum. The following year, Stamford resident Dr. G. R. R. Hertzberg revived the idea, gathering supporters and starting a fund drive, only to give up the effort when World War I began. Like a sapling rising from the roots, the idea poked its head above the ground still again in 1929, this time heralded by the Town Planning Commission—only to fizzle from lack of money.

None of which seemed to matter to John Ripley Forbes. In 1934, at age twenty-one, he was thrilled to hear of a meeting being called by Boy Scout executive A. Wilson Beeny to discuss reviving the museum idea. Aware of John's considerable skills, the group immediately appointed him curator, to be assisted by a host of other enthusiasts, mostly women, serving on committees with names like Ways and Means, Organization, Library Chairman, Exhibits, and Programs.

Until the early 1900s, respected museums—that is, those not inclined toward crude P. T. Barnum–style curiosities—thought of themselves as nothing less than the repositories of Western civilization. And repositories they were: dark, quiet cathedrals of secular culture; brick vaults lined with long runs of glass cases, each with a mind-numbing collection of specimens. Somber docents led visitors from room to room, talking in whispers. Such places were often less concerned with fostering intellect and curiosity than they were with simply serving those educated enough to already possess such qualities. Henry David Thoreau put it bluntly: "I hate museums, there is nothing so weighs upon my spirit. They are the catacombs of nature. One green bud of spring, one willow catkin, one faint trill from a migrating sparrow would set the world on its legs again. The life that is in a single green weed is of more worth than all this death." This dismal mold was ultimately broken open by nature museums in New York and Boston—in particular, those created for children. Under John's guiding hand, the mold would be broken yet again in the town of Stamford.

To display their exhibits, John and his cohorts were able to secure a tiny stone shelter in Stamford's Cummings Park. Among the hundreds of items were pieces of the collection Forbes had amassed as a boy in the attic of his father's rectory, and later, in the basement of the Bruce Museum in Greenwich. Locals contributed personal mounts—everything from birds to monkeys to a large collection of more than 1,000 moths and butterflies. A small group of live animals rounded out the offerings. On the day the little stone house in Cummings Park opened its doors, July 4, 1934, children arrived in droves—eager not only to see the exhibits but to sign up for a long list of nature walks and wildlife programs being offered by Forbes and a volunteer named Ruth Powers. By August, in addition to a full slate of programs there were special lectures every other day—"The Porcupine and Its Habits," "Snakes of Stamford," "Stamford Bird Life"—most with either live animals or movies, the latter being for most a rare treat. So great was the response that kids were routinely turned away due to limited space. Seeing their disappointment, suffering their pouting, John got busy adding still more events.

At the end of any given day, after changing clothes and gulping down a quick meal, Forbes and Ruth Powers loaded the car with bird mounts and butterfly displays, and perhaps a snake or squirrel or rabbit or two, and drove off to conduct nature programs for various church and civic groups around the city. The meeting rooms were almost always packed with mothers and fathers holding the hands of children who seemed about to pass out with excitement. Forbes was even then a masterful presenter—warm but intense, quick to let out a booming laugh, more often than not leaving people feeling as if they were considering nature for the very first time. At the end of the evening, adults and kids alike streamed back out into the streets like religious converts, determined to spread the word. Which in turn brought still more speaking invitations, both in Stamford and in surrounding communities.

Meanwhile, collections at the little museum continued to grow. By summer's end Forbes had secured the loan of another 1,400 moths and butterflies; a head and horn exhibit consisting of five moose, three elk, two deer, two caribou, one horse, and one buffalo; a mineral collection from Anna Gallup at the Brooklyn Children's Museum; and 1,500 bird eggs, 4,000 plants, 160 bird skins, five paintings, twenty-five minerals, two additional shell collections, 200 books, 100 tropical and native birds, and one skunk. Dr. Hertzberg himself offered a fox and bear cub along with five fish, followed by insects, a bald eagle, rare shells, two loons, one deer head, three alligators, a red-shouldered hawk, one porcupine, and one each of wildcat, groundhog, and weasel. Yet the effort remained largely a labor of love. The organization's initial ledger from the First Stamford National Bank and Trust shows an opening deposit on July 11, 1934, of ninety dollars. Accompanying the ledger page is a brown, wrinkled piece of paper with pencil scribblings in John's handwriting, recording names and general addresses from local contributors: B. Mead from Webbs Hill, one dollar; Ms. Ryder (no address), fifty cents; another fifty cents from one Mr. Leete from the town of Greenwich.

Unfortunately, the health of both William Hornaday and A. Wilson Beeny was declining. As the men's energy and influence waned, Dr. Hertzberg began pushing hard to change the existing Children's Museum Association into the Stamford Natural History

Museum. John agreed to the name change reluctantly; down the road, though, he would come to regret it. A budget of $3,000 was set (about $45,000 in today's dollars)—half of which Forbes raised single-handedly. On June 27, 1936, the doors opened to a new facility, this one housed in three second-story rooms of the Stamford Trust Company bank building. "In a miraculously short time," wrote superintendent of schools Leon Staples, "the rooms . . . were filled with a well organized collection of specimens." He describes young Forbes, who was still serving as curator, as "an organizer, a speaker of much real ability, a traveler of some repute," and above all, a lover of humanity. "Somewhere he will fill a big position and his genius will blossom forth into splendid leadership."

Rare, it seems, is the man who can provide inspiration for an organization while at the same time laying down the intricacies of its infrastructure. But thanks in part to his close relationship with mentor William Hornaday, John was growing adept at both. Knowing that fledgling museum efforts often fell victim to lack of planning, Forbes developed detailed blueprints for how to make the program sustainable in the coming years. By the summer of 1936 he was cautioning the museum board about the "very great need for immediate organization if our museum is to continue. We have grown from a small group of people who met at our president's house last February to a large organization of some six hundred people." He called for an immediate revamping of the board of directors. Further, he declared, "a membership drive should be organized as soon as possible and our membership increased, especially the associate membership so we will have a supporting membership [as in primary benefactors] of at least 100."

By the time a year had passed in the new location, over 42,000 visitors had come through the museum's doors, more than 30,000 of them children. Achieving that kind of success in a small city meant a constant push by Forbes to change exhibits, invent new programs, and hustle motion pictures—in short, to keep things fresh enough that people wanted to keep coming back. At the same time, he worked doggedly to forge links with the community, including garden clubs, civic groups, and area schools. "Instead of each school's attempting to set up a little museum for itself," explained a reporter for the *Stamford Advocate*, "the single central museum provides a larger range of exhibits and is in charge of a specialist who knows his stuff."

In the end, however, John would be undone by something he was never willing to abide: a push by the president of the board, Dr. Hertzberg, to make Stamford's museum less targeted toward children. (Among other things, Hertzberg was adamantly opposed to live animals of any kind, whereas John saw them as a critical resource for attracting kids.) In August 1937 Forbes wrote a letter to friend Anna Billings Gallup at the Brooklyn Children's Museum, explaining his resignation as curator in advance of being fired. "I resigned," he wrote, "because I would no longer put up with the continued actions of our President and would under no conditions serve as the curator unless my program of a museum for the children was carried out." The president would need to resign, Forbes said. In fact, it was "his resignation or mine."

No museum not 100 percent committed to children could last in Stamford, John told Anna. With the current leadership it could be run only one way, and, Forbes wrote, "that is not the way I promised those who supported it financially." Writing also to the director of the Children's Museum in Hartford, Connecticut, John regretted that he wasn't able to convince the original backers to call the facility the Stamford Children's Museum, which he realized too late would have obligated them to keep children foremost in their programming.

Recalling the incident years later, John referred to himself as a "mildly upset kid"—though one who suddenly understood that sooner or later "you have to play politics."

Creating engaging natural history programs is a lot more complicated than most people think. The skills necessary simply to prepare mounts of animals—the taxidermy part of the job—take years to master. To prepare a single bird mount for display required making a careful incision in the back or chest and the wings and legs, then carefully removing the tissue and most of the bones. To prevent decay, a dry preservative was gently rubbed into the animal to absorb fat (cornmeal was long a favorite of John's for this), along with alum or a similar preservative. Finally, the shell of the bird was stuffed with cotton or foam—just enough (and in all the right places) for the creature to regain its natural shape, at which point it was sewed back together.

To refine these and other skills, including a long list of tricks for creating lifelike displays, after high school John packed his bags and headed to the University of Iowa. It was not only one of the best schools in the nation for curators—indeed, it had the oldest continuously offered museum training program in the country—but the guy in charge, Homer Dill, was a former protégé of William Hornaday. Dill maintained a research collection of some 30,000 bird skins and eggs, several thousand mammal skins, and an extensive assortment of fish and marine invertebrates. In 1909 he'd made a reputation by assembling the bones of a whale into a skeletal exhibit—a daunting task made more difficult by the existence of fewer than a dozen such assembled skeletons in the entire world. Month after month, with students working by Dill's side, the assembly took shape, jaw pieces and ribs and spinal column and intervertebral discs—some two tons of bones in all—carefully fitted back together until they once again became the framework of a whale.

John's coursework included classes in collecting and mounting, as well as the use of natural models to construct leaves, grass, and flowers for habitat displays. He attended zoology labs and clay modeling classes, where he learned to sculpt perfect anatomical replicas of various animals and birds. And there was always more taxidermy. Moose or bison were prepared by first exposing the bones to flesh-eating beetles, then reassembling the skeleton using metal rods and wire armature. (Even today, tanks full of the dermestid beetle remain a staple at many museums.) Onto the armature were then spread thin layers of clay, one after another, painstakingly sculpted into exactly the right musculature to fit the skeleton. From this model, plaster molds were made and then covered with tightly stretched animal hide. In short, such work required the steady hands of a surgeon and the eye of a sculptor, not to mention an intimate knowledge of the bones of countless species.

With a year of studies under his belt, and following a brief stint at the Boston School of Fine Arts, Forbes turned his attention to entering still another university, this time to focus on wildlife biology. Not surprisingly, he chose William Hornaday's alma mater, Bowdoin College in Brunswick, Maine, notable in part for the work of celebrated ornithologist Albert Gross. Highly regarded for his work with ruffed grouse and the heath hen, by his death in 1970 Gross had penned a staggering 250 books and scientific articles. And much like Hornaday, Professor Gross found something especially intriguing about young John Forbes.

Given the highly competitive nature of Bowdoin, John's lackluster academic performance in certain "less interesting" classes at Iowa meant doing some fast footwork if he was to have any chance of being accepted. In a letter to the Bowdoin admissions board, he did his best to explain the unpleasant fact of a failing grade in zoology at the University of Iowa.

> During the second term I did some extra work in organizing a large entomological collection. As a result of this I found I was not able to give the time necessary for a fine Zoology course I had signed for. On advice of the professor I dropped out of the subject so as to give the proper attention to this work. I desire to take the rest of the course at Bowdoin. I am explaining this as I expect there will be some question when the records are sent and zoology for the second term is marked failure. I did not go through the official red tape in that it would involve too much unpleasantness and my instructor felt it was not needed as I was not interested in marks or degree but only in obtaining good results.

As convincing as Forbes could be, in the end it was almost certainly letters written by other supporters—Hornaday in particular—that swayed the admissions board. "I was first attracted to young Forbes," Hornaday wrote to Albert Gross, "by the private museum that he had constructed with his own boyish hands, on the strength of his own free observations in museums, and before he had received any instruction whatever in museology. John Forbes is not only a tremendous worker, but he has a fine sense of proportion, and the judgment that is so vitally necessary in the field that he is seeking

Among John's long list of honors and awards, the one he prized most was his honorary doctorate from Bowdoin College, which he received at age 73. "John loved the fact," says his wife Margaret, "that while most people tended to graduate from college in four years, it took him fifty."

to enter. I think that with Bowdoin as his Alma mater, he will go far." Gross was impressed, passing the letter on to Bowdoin president K. C. M. Sills: "Since there was some question concerning the admission of John Forbes as a student to Bowdoin," Gross told Sills, "the enclosed letter from Dr. Hornaday may be of interest."

John was at last accepted into Bowdoin. Yet, curiously, at the end of one feverish year of work he decided to move on. Even with such a short stay, however, the college would forever hold a special place in his heart. Among a long list of honors and awards garnered in the decades to come, his most prized of all was an honorary doctorate from Bowdoin, awarded when he was seventy-three in a ceremony that also presented doctorates to poet Maya Angelou and writer Robley Wilson Jr. "John loved the fact," says his wife, Margaret, "that while most people tended to graduate from college in four years, it took him fifty." In truth, the urge to so honor John had been brewing for some time—floated on at least two occasions by New York City commissioner of corrections and Bowdoin graduate Austin H. MacCormick. Few Americans, said MacCormick, had done more than Forbes to stimulate the development of future scientists. When the honor was finally bestowed, through a Doctor of Humane letters on May 23, 1987, it came with some generous words of praise.

> We honor you today because you did not keep what you found for yourself. You shared your excitement and enthusiasm and love of learning. To say that you established 20 museums and science centers and 12 nature sanctuaries around the country, and aided in the foundation of more than 200 other science centers is only to touch the surface of your achievement. What cannot be counted, but only felt and marveled at, is the way you have enriched so many young lives and set so many people on the path to distinguished scientific careers. The lessons in ecology you have taught will ensure that your work endures for future generations on this planet you love so well. You have been a great friend of the sciences and of education, and that other friend of science and patron of education, James Bowdoin III, would surely share our pleasure in saluting you today.

For the moment, though, such accomplishment was still a long way off. Between John's early studies and that honorary doctorate lay a long road through a thousand slices of nature, some big and some small, stretching to the top of the earth and across the continent. ✍

In the summer of 1937, Forbes left on a scientific expedition to the Arctic
aboard the ship Gertrude Thebaud, commanded by famed explorer Donald
MacMillan. Serving as both taxidermist and ornithologist for the expedition,
John's 215 Arctic bird specimens, collected for the Lee Museum at Bowdoin
College, would leave that school with one of the finest northern bird collections
in the nation.

Chapter Two

FIRE AND ICE

ON FIRST GLANCE, IT MIGHT SEEM that a fifteen-year-old kid who builds a full-blown natural history museum in the attic would be well on his way to becoming a full-fledged egghead. The superintendent of schools in Stamford, for one, liked to refer to John's "microscopic mind," as well as his ability to gather "encyclopedic information with great speed and accuracy." Yet what Forbes was up to in the peak of the St. Andrew's rectory was hardly just an exercise in intellect; indeed his activities weren't far removed from the doings of some of the most swashbuckling heroes of the day.

The early decades of the twentieth century were a time of unparalleled scientific exploration, the majority of it sponsored by museums. While John was out in his rowboat on Lake Winnipesaukee, following frogs along the inlets of Bear Island, Roy Chapman Andrews—the pistol-toting paleontologist whose life would give rise to a cinematic hero called Indiana Jones— was wandering the deserts of Mongolia, dodging bandits and stumbling through heat and sandstorms, searching for dinosaur eggs and missing links on yet another dangerous assignment for the American Museum of Natural History. As John graduated from high school, Richard Byrd was on his second trek to the Antarctic, where he would spend five brutal months alone in a tiny hut at 76 degrees below zero. (Harold June of Stamford had served as Byrd's copilot during his initial Antarctic expedition; in June 1930, when Forbes was seventeen, the city had given June a full-blown hero's welcome, touting him as "Stamford's Best-Known Traveler.") In short, for the properly curious and adventurous scientific-minded person of the day, right livelihood meant heading out to some far-flung corner of the wild, to one day return with boxes filled with new discoveries for the grand museums of the big cities.

John's first big chance to roam comes in the summer of 1937. Toward the end of June he bids farewell to New England from the stern rail of the *Gertrude Thebaud*, easing north out of Gloucester, Massachusetts, under a plump, butter-colored moon. Already well-known as a racing schooner, this time the *Thebaud* is on a seventy-two-day research journey to the Arctic, manned by a gaggle of eager though mostly inexperienced young men from Bowdoin College, Kirksville College, and New York University. Most are from families of means—future leaders from across the Northeast, soon to follow their fathers onto Wall Street and Madison Avenue and Beacon Hill. For them this is a rite of passage of sorts, a threshold between boyhood and manhood—something to recount in future years over fine dinners and glasses of port. For John, though, the voyage is something altogether different. At twenty-four he's come aboard as a scientist, assigned the task of collecting bird skins for the Lee Museum of Natural History at Maine's Bowdoin College. As exciting for him as the journey may be in itself, it's also a big step on the path of his chosen career.

Commanding the voyage—and in his own way no less committed to sharing his passion with young people than Forbes—is none other than Donald MacMillan, a superstar to sailors and landlubbers alike. Having lost his own father at sea at age nine, MacMillan is on his sixteenth trek to the Arctic, halfway through a forty-six-year career under sail. Before calling it quits after a final journey at age eighty, "Mac" will amass more than 300,000 miles by sea. Beyond mere experience he offers a unique brand of discipline and patience, qualities that grow even more solid in the face of pending disaster. Back near the turn of the century, on two consecutive nights he calmly saved the lives of nine people in two shipwrecks—a feat that caught the attention of famed Arctic explorer Robert Peary. Hugely impressed, Peary wasted no time sending an invitation for MacMillan to join his 1905 attempt on the North Pole. Alas, MacMillan was teaching at a seamanship-based summer camp for teens he'd started several years earlier, and refused to break his commitment to the boys.

MacMillan would gain another chance three years later when in 1908 Peary again set out for the North Pole. It was the lucky try for Peary, who finally made it on April 9. MacMillan fared less well, however, forced to abandon the effort when he froze the heels of his feet. Five years later, in 1913—the year John Ripley Forbes was born—thirty-nine-year-old MacMillan set off yet again for the far North, this time commanding his own expedition to Greenland. There he would be stranded for more than three years, finally rescued in 1917 by Robert Bartlett in the ship *Neptune*.

The early days of Forbes' 1937 journey with MacMillan are rife with murky weather, the fog growing so heavy that Newfoundland, lying just to port, remains invisible. Most nights the person on bow watch spends hour after hour turning the handle on the foghorn, sending mournful groans into the great unknown. To top it off there's been a rash of seasickness, sending more than half the crew heaving over the rails. Forbes, though, has no such problems, writing in a letter to his parents on July 1 that he "felt kind of sick once or twice but did not upchuck." One boy, he says, is both homesick and seasick, one night so bad off that the men had to tie him to his bunk.

Not just the boys are suffering. Chief ornithologist and Bowdoin professor Alfred Gross, as well as Professors Starrett, French, and Haines, are so sick that they have little idea what's going on, unable even to take their shifts on night watch. A week out of Gloucester, Alfred Gross finally gives up, leaving to make his way home to Brunswick by rail. Shortly before staggering off the ship, he hands the mantle of chief ornithologist for the expedition to his former student John Forbes.

For Forbes, simply getting on board the *Thebaud* required heroic effort. Having pestered Albert Gross countless times for a spot on the expedition—a request passed on numerous times to the commander—MacMillan finally wrote John in late May 1937, barely a month before the scheduled departure. "The expense of reequipping the *Thebaud* and for the 6,000 mile cruise of seventy days is so much more than we ever anticipated that we must have two or three more men at $750 each to pay all our bills. If you can manage to raise the money I feel quite sure that you will easily get it back through your lectures and your articles." MacMillan wrote again on June 15, telling Forbes he had reserved a bunk, "feeling quite sure that you would have no difficulty in raising the money. If you should fail to do so, it hardly gives me time to fill your place."

Though in years to come John would routinely rub elbows with some of the wealthiest people in the country, convincing them to commit millions of dollars to a wide range of nature preserves and children's museums, his own life could be better described as careening along the edges of financial calamity. Given his circumstances, raising $750 in a matter of weeks (equivalent to about $10,500 today) was an astonishing task—one most young men of such modest means would have considered out of the question.

When MacMillan's confirmation letter arrived, John started knocking on the doors of wealthy men, mostly Bowdoin graduates. He pitched hard, emphasizing that his role of official taxidermist for the voyage would directly benefit the Lee Museum, a shining star of their alma mater. With MacMillan's permission, he had letterhead printed with the commander's name on it, thereby lending credibility to what otherwise might have seemed little more than a brash if charming scheme. John also tried to reassure the dubious by inviting them to send their checks to Albert Gross, in the name of the college, rather than directly to him. Acting on a lead from Thomas Lamont in his hometown of Stamford, John first tracked down Bowdoin graduate Harvey Gibson, cajoling him into making a whopping $100 contribution. More donations followed, mostly from New York.

By June 11 John had $400 in pledges. "It's some task," he admitted in a letter to Alfred Gross, "but I expect to have raised the full amount by the end or middle of next week." Gross was astonished. "I wish that I had your ability to raise funds," he lamented in his return letter. In fact, John's struggle to reach the Arctic provides one of the earliest glimpses of his uncanny knack for raising money. In the years to follow he would employ similar, if arguably more refined, acts of nudging and cajoling, using them with donors from Laurance Rockefeller to Averill Harriman to *Reader's Digest* founder DeWitt Wallace. On numerous occasions he would claim that beating the bushes to give kids a chance to be out in nature was among his favorite things to do. And furthermore, that it was a great service to help people with lots of money figure out a truly worthwhile way to spend it.

Because of the Great Depression, most of the men John contacted for the Arctic journey were considerably less well heeled than they'd once been. Besides that, many Bowdoin alumni were, as usual, away from New York for the summer, hiding out in cooler, quieter retreats in the north. Slightly desperate, on June 19 Forbes wrote to Hoyt Moore, a New York attorney and Bowdoin alumnus who had already pledged $50 toward the $750 goal; John asked for $50 more. Moore responded right away, clearly miffed, saying how $100 was more than his share. Still, in the end he acquiesced. In his accompanying note, Moore wrote: "It is so late that there is now no time to collect the balance from others and I, accordingly, am enclosing herewith my check to the order of Bowdoin College—for MacMillan Arctic Expedition." Forbes also invited Bowdoin graduate Harvey Gibson, of Manufacturers Trust in New York, to double down. Like Moore, he found it impossible to say no.

While fund-raising with one hand, with the other John decided to test the waters with MacMillan to see whether he might come down from his $750 fee—an idea first suggested in passing by Albert Gross. Given that he'd be preparing skins for the commander's old college, Forbes suggested in a letter, maybe it would be appropriate to trim off $250 or so. After mailing the letter, Forbes wrote another one to Albert

John in 1937 at twenty-four, bound for the Arctic aboard the Gertrude Thebaud. *Forbes initially signed on for the voyage as a taxidermist. An early departure due to illness of Bowdoin ornithology professor Albert Gross, though, led to Forbes also taking over as the expedition's chief ornithologist.*

Gross, telling him how sure he was that MacMillan would help. "After all," wrote John, "I am not going as a student but as a member of the staff, and to work for the college and MacMillan himself."

MacMillan refused to budge. In the end Forbes nearly made it, gleaning $535, mostly from the men in New York, but also small amounts from various family friends. In a last anxious move he pledged his car as collateral against what he owed. And with that he was off. The third week of June found him hustling north across New England, stopping in Boston just long enough to pick up motion picture film for the expedition, arriving at the ship in Portland, Maine, at 2:45 p.m., fifteen minutes before she left the docks.

This isn't Forbes' first sea voyage, though it is by far his most ambitious. Two years earlier, in 1935, he'd climbed aboard the forty-two-foot vessel *Eider Duck* for six days of Biological Survey work along the Maine Coast assessing island bird populations. In letters to his parents he showed himself to be thoroughly in his element, declaring on the fifth day at sea that he'd never had such a wonderful time. He chronicled ospreys feeding their young high up in a tree and kingfishers plucking dinner from the water. He listened to the veery thrush, the black-throated green warbler, and the nighthawk. In all, he wrote, "it gives me an idea of the opportunities of work in ornithology and more than ever convinces me that ornithology is my field and that's that." He detailed accounts of onshore explorations, including counting 1,481 gull eggs on Elm Island, noting with great detail variations in their size and color. In an aside, he talked about Elm Island being for sale by one Hiram P. Fallow of Rockland, Maine. "It would make an excellent bird sanctuary and life history research station," he told his parents. "What a fine island for the Maine Audubon society."

But the trip to the Arctic is proving more exciting still. After spotting whales crossing the Strait of Belle Isle, Forbes notes a vast array of grumpers, murres, gammets, and puffins appearing, the stubby wings of the latter barely able to lift them off the water before the advancing ship. In the first two weeks of the voyage, he will log sixty bird species, including twenty he's never seen before.

Beyond Isle au Haut, the ship breaks a run of phosphorescence, causing the sea to light up, glistening in graceful arcs beyond the stern like a river of cool fire. Day by day the coastal villages decrease in number, becoming more remote. Point Armour has just fifteen buildings, all painted white, housing only two dozen villagers, more than half of them children. It's John's first encounter with subsistence culture, the villagers making their livings mostly by fishing for cod and herring and salmon and selling it in Newfoundland. Some trap silver fox, caribou, and seals for the Hudson's Bay Company, more often than not selling them for a tiny fraction of their real worth. A preacher, Forbes learns, comes to Point Armour twice a year, though on most days God floats in on the airwaves, courtesy of radio station CFCY in Quebec. The mail comes every three weeks. Winter brings snow ten feet deep. By all indications cigarettes are the ultimate luxury, so much so that whenever they appear, the entire village, including small children, lights up with relish.

Later on, in the village of Nain, Labrador, on sighting the approaching *Thebaud*, the villagers call their brass band down to shore, where they serenade the ship and crew into port with strains of "Abide with Me." The locals are quick to grow sullen, though, on learning that their favorite motion picture from a previous visit, *Mickey Mouse*, didn't make it onto the ship.

Beyond the exquisite puzzle of northern flora and fauna, beyond the native cultures that continue to fascinate at every turn, on most days Forbes and his shipmates are awash in lonely, haunting natural beauty: red sunsets falling on water the color of plum pudding; icebergs floating in the distance; jumbles of splintered rock softened by patches of skunk currant and willow and alder. John's shipmate Walter Staples relates in a letter to his parents that people had probably landed on only one out of a hundred of the cold, windswept islands passing on either side of the ship. "Regardless of the uselessness of it and the necessity of remaining in rags for life-times," he says, "I can understand why men live here. And I'll bet they are happy."

In the last days of July, at York Sound, the crew anchors near the prow of Grinnell Glacier, off-loading several teams of students and scientists to make their way to the upper reaches of the ice field. Absent any real climbing plan—some traveling on skis and some by foot—the various parties break apart, scattering across the glacier. They at first seem unaware of the dangers posed by the gaping crevasses incised across the ice field. Then, without warning, student Charles Edwards slips on the ice and falls into a crevasse. By no small miracle he manages to stop his headlong tumble partway down, holding on long enough for the rest of the crew to manage a rescue. He later writes in his diary not about the terror of almost dying but about the "bare, untouched natural beauty" of the abyss.

In the wee hours of an Arctic morning off Baffin Island, at Frobisher Bay, the luck runs dry. Anchored just west of the Labrador Sea, around three in the morning the several dozen young men slumbering under the wooden decks of the schooner are awakened by the growl of the ship's engine. This time, though, something's off-kilter—a throbbing of revving and pausing, revving and pausing. Then, silence. Twenty minutes later, in the murky light of predawn, the boys rouse to a gruff shout from the bow calling for all hands on deck. Chattering nervously, they shove legs and arms into pants and shirts and scurry up through the forward hatch.

The gargantuan tidal flows of Frobisher Bay, rushing outbound to the sea, have dropped the sixty-foot schooner like a stone, grounding the beam against a massive slab of rock. As the water level falls, the ship begins groaning, listing, then finally heaving sharply to port. Cook Charlie Crocker doesn't bother hiding his worry. Around 4:30 in the morning he shakes his head, turns to young Walter Staples, and says, "I've seen ships like this before. She's gone for sure." And

At remote Frobisher Bay, at the southeast corner of Baffin Island, extreme tides left the Gertrude Thebaud *marooned, forcing Commander Donald MacMillan to send the only SOS radio message of his long career.*

with that he stuffs his belongings into a seabag, pulls on his oilskins, hops over the leeward rail, and wades to shore.

The nearest chance for help lies with a small band of Inuit villagers, just now arriving at their summer fishing grounds thirty miles across the bay. To reach them means a dangerous passage in a fifteen-foot motor launch and seven tiny dories, navigating both drifting ice and ferocious, thirty-foot tides. Meanwhile, the government outpost on Resolution Island is more than 100 miles distant, with few protected anchorages. As for being spotted by another ship, even if one happens by the chances are slim that its crew would sight the *Thebaud* in this hidden nook. Although the food supply can probably be stretched to two months, most of the boys traveling with MacMillan have little suitable clothing for autumn in the Arctic.

The *Thebaud* continues to list. Before long, seams in the ship's planking start to break open, mostly in the vicinity of the commander's cabin, allowing water to pour in through quarter-inch gaps. By low tide the vessel hangs precariously, cocked at thirty-five degrees, and icy water is slopping over the rails and beginning to fill the hold. Anticipating massive flooding when the tide returns, Captain Jack Crowell assembles the boys into a frenzied chain of workers, stuffing clothing and equipment into pillowcases and handing the bundles up through the hatch, where they're ferried first by dory and then by foot to the nearby shore. Fueled by quick gulps of jam and crackers, the boys race against the inbound tide—now rising at an incredible rate of more than four and a half feet every hour. Hustling furiously in the dining room, a group of boys watches as first chairs and salt and pepper shakers float by, followed by maps and books, films and playing cards. Most troubling of all, though, also in the drink are hundreds of plant and egg specimens gathered during the voyage, as well as a number of John Forbes' precious bird skins.

Though almost no one knows it, MacMillan has just ordered the radioman to send an SOS, saying all hands are abandoning the *Thebaud* to make their way to Resolution Island. In all his years spent roaming the Arctic, this is the only distress call MacMillan will ever send. But due either to the ship's location or to weak batteries in the radio, no one will ever hear it.

Back in Stamford, with no mail service from the crew for several weeks, family and friends are wondering how young Forbes is faring.

For years they've watched with amazement this young museum man in the making, beginning all the way back when they came to see his nature exhibits in that muggy, airless attic of the Episcopalian rectory. So too have they come to know him through his writings, which for years have been appearing regularly in local newspapers and regional publications of the Audubon Society. By the time John was sixteen, his Audubon writings in particular seemed to suggest the elegant eye of a naturalist:

One day while taking my usual bird walk in New Hampshire, on an island in the middle of Lake Winnipesaukee, I was coming near the lagoon. This is a place sheltered from storms, a place where boats are kept. I thought I would take my rowboat and look for hawks and ducks, since I had found no luck this morning on the land. As I was rowing out I saw, to my great surprise, two large birds flying overhead. It was about 6:30 in the morning. Keeping more quiet, I rowed out of the lagoon with my boat and field glasses when suddenly a large form swept down from the air within two feet of my boat, then took to the air as fast as it came.

For some moments I stood as one greatly surprised. As this large form swept down, I saw as plainly as day the huge white head and the white tail. I never realized before that the eagle was so very large. I had often seen them up in the sky but never so close. This bird deserves the title, "The King of Birds."

Knowing well his proficiency with nature, John's high school teachers and fellow students routinely came to him with injured or

Though led by famed Arctic explorer Donald MacMillan, the crew of "Mac's" seventy-two day voyage to the Arctic in 1937 was made up mostly of college students from the Northeast. A dangerous grounding of the ship at Frobisher Bay damaged John's valuable bird mount collection, leaving him to spend much of the return trip salvaging specimens. "That at least can be said for [John]," wrote fellow ship mate Walter Staples. "He has stuck faithfully with his work and did not get discouraged."

suffering animals. One day early in the school year, a science teacher approached Forbes with a worried look on his face, having overheard another boy talking about accidentally catching a "red-shouldered" hawk in a trap. The bird was now apparently starving to death. When at last the final bell of the school day rang, Forbes ran to the boy's house, where he looked the injured bird over, flipped the boy a hard-earned dollar, then gently lifted the weakened creature into a basket and headed for home.

Back at the rectory, John placed the hawk in a box big enough to allow it to spread its wings. Then he began a patient, persistent effort to feed it—approaching quietly, gently laying down raw chunks of beef, and withdrawing. By the end of the week, the bird's foot had healed and the hawk was showing a new flush of strength. Soon afterward, "Bill," as John called the bird, was released in the backyard—rising in circles with great flaps of his wings, finally floating off toward the wooded edges of town.

In a later conversation with the boy who'd caught the bird, John learned that during an early feeding attempt the boy had put a dead chicken in the coop but the hawk wouldn't touch it. "This was worthy proof," John noted, "that the Red Shouldered Hawk is innocent of deserving the false name 'Chicken Hawk.'"

At Frobisher Bay, with the *Gertrude Thebaud* still marooned on the rocks, things are going from bad to worse. "The seams on the port side were wide open," Charles Edwards would later write, "and a river of water pouring through various leaks. She was filling fast, and all hope for her was gone." Then, to everyone's astonishment, at around six in the morning the ship begins to right itself on the incoming tide. With a boisterous shout Captain Crowell calls the crew from their feverish attempts at salvage, setting them instead to the job of trying to get the water out. The boys pump and bail with all their might, hour after hour. "The water had reached the ceiling on the port side and was up to the cabin house," noted a student named Milton, "when suddenly the glad cry 'she's rising' sprung out. We at once went to the pumps, opened her hold and with a tackle and water buckets took out water at the rate of at least 20,000 gallons for four hours, and the hand pumps going six hours. We got her dry at two o'clock." At three thirty in the afternoon, Charlie the cook rewarded the boys with a hot meal of beans and corned beef.

Yet despite this good turn of events, a northwest wind continues to hold the ship against the rocks. Disaster is still close at hand, especially if the tide runs out again without the crew being able to first brace the hull. The engine is useless, out of commission since being submerged when the hold flooded. In a desperate move, Captain Crowell orders the tiny fifteen-foot motor launch to be tethered to the *Thebaud*. With the launch pulling against a brisk wind—one growing stronger by the minute—the schooner rocks, groans, and finally comes free. Clear of imminent danger, the jumbo jib is hoisted and catches wind, and at last the *Thebaud* begins tracking a line toward Sandy Bay. "If we hadn't been so tired," Walter Staples says, "I think we might have cheered."

At this point Captain Crowell, who'd traveled with MacMillan several times in years past, immediately makes plans to set sail for Gloucester or some other port, where the ship can be hauled out and thoroughly inspected. "I was first amazed when Admiral MacMillan took me aside and said 'Jack, I have promised to take these people up to the Arctic Circle.'" A properly cautious sailor, Crowell needs to chew on the idea for a while but in the end agrees to continue the journey. So on they go, with the young crew feeling more seasoned by their close call with disaster—first to Brewster Point for a week of exploring and collecting, then north to the Arctic Circle. And finally south, homeward bound.

For Forbes especially, though, the accident at Frobisher Bay isn't entirely over. Two boxes containing more than seventy bird skins were washed about during the flooding of the ship; many have been badly damaged. For much of the week following the grounding, he will spend every waking hour redoing what he'd done in the initial weeks of the voyage, by no small miracle managing to save most of the specimens. "Those badly damaged," he later noted, "were saved as scientific records by placing them in alcohol solution. When the finished skins were again fixed and packed away a count of the damage revealed but five birds had been lost during the flood."

His dogged determination would earn John no small respect from the other boys. "That at least can be said for [John]," Walter Staples wrote in his journal. "He has stuck faithfully with his work and did not get discouraged when he lost some of his birds and a great deal of his equipment with the flood." More than once Forbes worked through the night, Staples added, trying to "get caught up with all of the work that has gotten ahead of him." By the end of the journey even MacMillan was impressed, declaring that Forbes worked as hard as any man on board. Even with the near disaster, John's gathering of 215 Arctic birds, including the rare Greenland wheatear, would garner Bowdoin one of the best collections of northern bird specimens in the nation. He also returned with 150 pages of notes and 100 more pages of hard data.

On returning home, John wrote to noted zoologist Wynne Edwards, sharing important observations he'd made in the Arctic on guillemots. In the letter he offered to work up the data and credit it to Albert Gross, who'd been investigating guillemot subspecies for some time. After reading the letter, Edwards wrote to Gross, asking the ornithologist to think about letting Forbes go ahead and run with any scientific articles on his own—a privilege that would, among other things, require John to examine a lot of skins in a lot of museums. "He is keen to make capital out of his first opportunity, and if he does not have the chance to write up and publish his guillemot studies, there is not a single item of scientific information worth publishing in the entire summer's work. I feel very strongly that he should be encouraged to proceed, with your aid."

Albert Gross wholeheartedly agreed.

Although John returned from the Arctic more on fire than ever, he was at the same time pushing against a heavy melancholy brought by having lost his dear friend and mentor William Hornaday the previous spring. Writing to Alfred Gross on April 18, two months before the ship sailed, John declared that he'd "just lost one of the best friends I have in the world." Barely had funeral services ended—attended by "many very prominent men"—before John was hatching plans to erect a memorial nature museum. In February 1938 he wrote a letter to President Franklin D. Roosevelt, a friend and great admirer of Hornaday, asking whether one of the new national parks being created at the time might be named after the famed zoologist. Roosevelt wrote back, pointing out that naming a national park after an individual was not in keeping with current policy. Still, wrote the president, "as I reflect upon the nature of Dr. Hornaday's splendid accomplishments in the field of conservation, remembering that he distinguished himself particularly by his leadership in safeguarding the American bison and various other forms of native wildlife from extinction, I am inclined to agree that some natural feature of our country should bear his name." The president went on to tell Forbes of several prominent peaks within Yellowstone National Park overlooking the bison range of the Lamar Valley. And so it happened that a certain rugged, brilliant mountain in the northeastern corner of Yellowstone came to be known as Hornaday Peak, towering high above what even today remains critical bison winter range.

Then, in yet another tribute to his friend and mentor, John went to work establishing the William T. Hornaday Memorial Fund, dedicated to sharing the wonders of the outdoors with children. At the time, no one (or at least no one but John Ripley Forbes) had the slightest inkling that the organization would become the driving force behind a feverish planting of children's nature museums and preserves across America. ❦

Chapter Three

MUSEUM MAN

BACK IN NEW ENGLAND FOLLOWING HIS VOYAGE to the Arctic—
desperate to pay the rent, as well as pay off the more than $200 he
still owed Commander MacMillan—John got busy writing a series
of articles he'd plotted aboard the *Gertrude Thebaud*, ultimately
placing several pieces in various scientific journals. When not
sitting at the typewriter, he was working diligently to set up lectures
meant to chronicle that grand journey to the Far North. Knowing
how important such speaking engagements would be to her son's
income, Forbes' mother had written a letter while he was still on
board the ship, advising him to ask MacMillan how much to charge
for a lecture. She wondered if $50 would be about right. Then she
cautioned John to "say no to the people who will ask you to do it for
nothing when you first get home."

Knowing that MacMillan was deeply pleased with his work in the
Arctic, John tried again to soften up the commander on the matter of
money. In a letter to MacMillan on September 6, 1937, he wondered

whether there might be some value in having done the work Dr. Gross had been supposed to do before leaving the expedition early due to illness. What's more, John explained, all the skins collected for the Lee Museum at Bowdoin, and many others besides, could be made available for MacMillan's own museum in Provincetown.

Once again, though, Mac refused to budge. "When others were sending in applications and making inquiries, and your place on the accepted list was in doubt—you assured me that you would go and that you would pay me the $750. I had faith in you and believed that you would, and therefore assured everyone that our list was complete. I could have accepted $750 for your place last May."

In the end, another $175 came in for Forbes through Professor Gross at Bowdoin College—late-arriving bounty from John's earlier calls for contributions from former alumni. This left him owing just $75. John expressed in a letter to the commander his fervent hope that the money would be forthcoming, even offering to borrow it from the bank, which MacMillan dismissed. Not understanding the way John had moved mountains to raise the initial funds, MacMillan felt sure he could raise such an amount "in a few weeks." At any rate, wrote MacMillan, "I trust your word and know that you will pay it when you can."

Again, though, while in years to come Forbes would be all but swimming in other people's money, in his own life he stayed tethered to a shoestring. It was nine years later, in 1946, when he finally sent MacMillan a check for the last $75. "I had forgotten all about it," Mac responded. "It will help me to re-equip [the ship] *Bowdoin* after her strenuous years in the service."

In early November 1937, John wrote his insurance agent, telling him to remove all coverage except fire and theft. "I know in the winter with these hills covered with ice and snow one would be foolish to run about in a car even if they could afford it for the danger is great. This will save me about fifty dollars which will help matters a good deal." Lacking the funds to travel, he also missed Christmas with the family that year, for the first time in his life. He begged temporary relief for a $2.50 debt he owed his father, explaining in a letter that he was "strapped to the limit at least until the middle of January." He also wrote that he hoped any Christmas gifts, especially money, could be sent to him as soon as possible, given the long list of speaking obligations awaiting him in the early weeks of January. "I will even take the dreaded tie," he told his father, "for a new tie can be used."

Yet lack of money did nothing to slow Forbes' work as a naturalist, including preparing the bird skins from the Arctic for Bowdoin's Lee Museum; making regular trips to the American Museum of Natural History to look up data on two Arctic birds of special interest, the guillemot and the Greenland wheatear; and finally, responding to Alfred Gross's suggestion that he try to unravel the "fine problem" of the bank swallow. "We know very little of the details of the life history of this bird," Gross told Forbes. "I am anxious to see you work out a technique which will enable you to study [their] home life."

Although the worst effects of the Great Depression were beginning to wane, people's hopes lifting a bit on the back of the New Deal, the job outlook in much of the country remained dismal. In the years since John started high school, the average family income in America had fallen by 40 percent, tumbling from $2,300 to just $1,500. Shanty towns called Hoovervilles, so named for the president who had assured the public that relief was best left to the private sector, were still scattered about the nation—sad tumbles of makeshift shelters fashioned from scrap metal and box wood, from old tires and cardboard, clustered in major urban areas from the nation's capital to the Pacific coast. In New York City alone, more than 65,000 homeless children still wandered the streets.

Yet, armed with the kind of heroic vision that often graces youth, John was sure the right work would come. Working to his favor was the fact that, compared to other institutions, museums were having an easier time than most. During the depression years, museum attendance had actually increased—in some places dramatically— as more and more working-class people passed through the doors for the first time. (By the time Forbes left Bowdoin, every city in America with more than 250,000 people had a museum.) It was in fact this surge by average families that helped push museums out of their lingering bad habit of creating extravagant displays for the wealthy. Suddenly, curators were scrambling to turn their facilities into places of general learning.

Wealthy benefactors—such as the Rockefeller and Carnegie Foundations, as well as Andrew Mellon, all of whom had lost enormous sums during the depression—actually donated more money to museums in the 1930s than they had during the raucous, freewheeling decade of the 1920s. This recharged commitment to philanthropy led not only to the expansion of existing facilities but also to the creation of dozens of small satellite museums, each carefully positioned to be available to average working families. At the same time, the Public Works Administration was setting aside more than $6 billion in federal funds to engage unemployed men and women in various projects for the public good. Much of the money went to museums.

Armed with letters of recommendation from William Hornaday and Albert Gross, John set his sights on two jobs in particular. The first was a position as curator of birds at the new Staten Island

Zoological Society. The second, and the one he ended up taking, was a low-paying position at Cornell, serving as assistant to stockbroker-turned-ornithologist Albert Brand. In the spring of 1929, the Fox-Case Movietone Company had come to Cornell looking for help recording bird songs on motion picture film. (At the time, motion picture film was by far the best medium for recording sound.) The crew spent a long morning in Ithaca recording a song sparrow, a rose-breasted grosbeak, and a house wren, but the results were dismal. Brand, having deep pockets from his former life on Wall Street, was eager to invest in better, lighter equipment. Over the next two years he and undergraduate assistant Peter Keane recorded more than forty birds in the field. To their great frustration, however, the quality remained poor.

Brand turned next to a cadre of electrical engineers to rebuild the equipment, making it both less cumbersome and more sensitive. At the suggestion of Peter Keane, who'd been intrigued by sound reflectors he'd seen at the newly constructed Radio City Music Hall in New York City, Brand further boosted the effort by employing parabolic technology. By the time Forbes came on board as Brand's assistant, the team had already crisscrossed the country on two major film and sound recording treks, capturing sights and sounds of several birds then hurtling toward extinction, including the California condor and the ivory-billed woodpecker.

Forbes cleared only fifteen dollars a week, though he had both cheap lodging and the use of a car. "I know you were worried that I had accepted some sort of a handy man's position," he wrote his parents in the fall of 1937, "which of course is not the case. You must realize that I would not have accepted this job unless it was a step forward. I never believe in taking a step backward."

But in truth, he was in over his head. Over the next two months it became increasingly clear that what Brand needed was someone not just with ornithology skills, which Forbes had in spades, but with the talents of an engineer. Despite having done cursory work with a Kodak film machine in the Arctic, John found such mechanical challenges beyond him. "Brand and I have come to the conclusion," he wrote to Alfred Gross, "that for his sake as well as my own I had better get back into the museum and lecture field which I seem to be better equipped for."

Shortly before coming to Cornell, John had heard of a strange circumstance unfolding half a country away, in Kansas City, Missouri. There a wealthy timber baron had died without warning, leaving a sprawling, rundown, Beaux-Arts classical-style home known as the Long Mansion to a city with absolutely no idea what to do with it. But John knew. And the way he figured it, all he had to do was convince a group of powerful urbanites from the Show-Me State who'd gathered to ponder the fate of the Long Mansion, not one of whom had ever heard his name. In the fall of 1939 John wrote two passionate letters to the Kansas City Museum Association board, both to no avail. So on a cold day in November, the former Eagle Scout decided to take matters into his own hands, loading up his Ford and steering it onto Highway 6, heading west.

Kansas City would never be the same. ✎

Chapter Four

A WHIRLWIND IN KANSAS

KANSAS CITY MUSEUM ASSOCIATION president Arthur W. Archer, like most of his colleagues, had a bad feeling he was in deep water. Though it's true that by 1939 natural history museums were common fare, in much of the country civic leaders were only beginning to see their real potential—not just as a means of kindling civic pride but as centers of education. While the Long Mansion was on one hand a glorious gift to the city, it would take phenomenal sums of money, management expertise, and marketing savvy to make it a prized institution. Overwhelmed, Archer headed for the East Coast, desperate for a little tutoring.

Among the leaders he sought out was the brilliant Mildred Manter, director of the Boston Children's Museum, at the time one of the finest facilities of its kind anywhere in the world. Besides offering Archer technical advice, Manter enthusiastically recommended a certain part-time employee named John Ripley Forbes, whom she'd come to know over the previous six months. On June 30, 1939, she wrote to Archer, suggesting Forbes as a great choice to lend a hand in Kansas City. Showing just how green he was to the whole idea of educational museums, Archer wrote back thanking her for the courtesy, suggesting that her kindness—as well as that of others in the field—"inspired me toward the belief that these museums must be really worthwhile."

But John Forbes wasn't the kind of guy to wait around to be asked. John knew of Manter's efforts on his behalf, and her letter had barely cooled in Archer's hands before another one arrived from young Forbes. It read in part: "As you may gather from Miss Manter, I have been very much interested in the Children's Museum movement, and am at the present time serving as the director of the William T. Hornaday Memorial Fund, which I have organized to bring about the establishment of more such museums." This was followed by a summary of Forbes' related experiences, which in truth seemed too vast for a man only in his twenties.

The following week Archer wrote a cautious letter to Forbes, explaining that the association had no money, let alone the sort of solid plan that would need to be in place before hiring outside help. Days later, in a letter dated August 22, 1939, John suggested Archer's hatchling group might drum up excitement for their project by using museum-oriented motion pictures, which Forbes could help arrange. By showing such films to "civic clubs, women's clubs, various organizations," as well as to "wealthy individuals in their homes," the group would not only stir interest but also establish the very infrastructure it needed for financial support. Sensing that Archer was clearly overwhelmed—and at the same time, growing nervous about his own job prospects—John included in this early correspondence four letters of recommendation as well as the names of several other people who could write on his behalf. The tone of his letters was effusive and confident—intended to give Archer the sense that if John wasn't exactly the light at the end of the tunnel, he was at least a reliable handrail to guide the group out of the darkness.

But the rock wouldn't budge. Archer responded several weeks later, this time explaining that as the association was still struggling with title to the mansion, it was in no position to employ a curator. Most young men would have let it rest and maybe tried again in a few months. But John responded right away, this time sweetening the pot: "The one fact I should like to stress is simply this: I should like to help with the initial plans, raising of funds, layout of building, arrangement of exhibits, organization of departments, etc. so important in launching a new museum." He went on to point out that both the Boston Children's Museum and the Brooklyn Children's Museum started out in one room, with little or no finances. Forbes wrote: "In the Boston Museum, the Director left a good position with promise of but one month's salary, to start what is now the largest museum of its kind in the world." Citing the strong confidence those in the museum field had in the public's enthusiasm for such projects, he told Archer that he himself had worked as a volunteer for five months, implying that he was willing to do so again.

At the end of this letter John offered to come to Kansas City at his own risk—with perhaps a two- or three-month salary arranged by the museum association—to immediately set about contacting outstanding financial prospects for critical pledges. He assured Archer: "I am very willing to take any risk necessary by coming out to Kansas City on such a short time basis, for I feel certain of the ultimate success of your project. Certainly if others have left good positions to develop museums with little or no salary, I think I am doing little indeed in making you this offer."

But the museum board, composed mostly of conservative

businessmen, couldn't bring themselves to take such an unconventional step. Archer wrote to John again in October, telling him that the drive for museum funds was stalled and that any related work would have to be put off until early 1940. In the meantime John had landed the position with Albert Brand at Cornell, though it would be only weeks before he understood he didn't have the technical skills to make it there. Obsessed with the Long Mansion, John speculated that the right donors were probably already in place and the only thing needed was someone to light a fire under them. If he couldn't convince Archer's team through the mail, he'd resort to more drastic measures. So in November he borrowed $100, packed a couple bags, bid farewell to friends and family, and headed for Missouri. Driving hard through a bleak midwestern landscape long past harvest, he arrived late on a Wednesday evening, caught three hours of sleep, then headed directly to the museum association office. There he stood before a befuddled Archer, asking to be put on the agenda for the next board meeting, which he knew was scheduled for that very afternoon.

At the board meeting, "I introduced myself and offered to work at first for nothing," Forbes later wrote, "until I had raised enough funds to cover the necessary expenses for the start of the work, if they would just give me a chance." He stressed to the board members how much they would benefit from a professional man like himself being on board, especially right then, when there was a need both to protect the collections and artifacts already in hand and to address the various structural and design issues with the mansion. With his skills at their disposal, John encouraged, the board was certain to get off on the right foot, creating exactly the kind of early success that would help attract more support down the road. He closed his remarks by asking to meet with them again the following week, at which point he would present concrete plans and suggestions for their consideration. The board was delighted though still suspicious. In the end, however, they figured there was nothing to lose.

John returned the following Thursday with a detailed summary of critical issues facing the museum, along with a list of specific tasks to be carried out in the weeks ahead. Years later, some of the board members admitted they hardly knew what had hit them. By unanimous vote Forbes was appointed supervisor without salary, to take effect December 1, after which he would be paid the meager sum of $100 a month—at least as long as he managed to raise the funds. With smiles and nods and handshakes all around, John jumped back into his Ford and drove home to Connecticut. There he tied up a few loose ends, reloaded his car, and headed again for the Midwest, showing up in Kansas City on the first morning of December, raring to go.

By anyone's definition the Long Mansion is extraordinary, with its seventy-two sprawling rooms wrapped in Indiana limestone and copper, perched on three acres high above the Missouri River Valley at Scarritt Point. Yet splendid as it might have been, by the time John shows up in December 1939 the estate has been vacant for six years—more than enough time to have tumbled into full-blown disrepair. Many of the valuables have been auctioned off. Salvage workers have been hard at work tearing apart portions of the building—removing fixtures, doors, moldings, and other items, often damaging walls and breaking plaster in the process, leaving the interior looking thoroughly ransacked. Dirt and dust and rubble are everywhere.

In the early weeks after John's arrival, the museum association continues to be wracked with anxiety, as if they'd walked into a burning building with a sprinkling can, desperate to figure out where best to pour the water first. They're also overwhelmed by having recently received as a gift thousands of items from the city's primary museum, housed at the Kansas City Public Library—treasures that include the magnificent Daniel Burns Dyer Collection of Native American artifacts as well as Missouri Valley Historical Society collections, the latter of which had been unceremoniously dumped on the second and third floors of the mansion shortly before John arrived. One board member suggests the first order of business should be to hire moving trucks to cart the highly fragile library collection over to the mansion to be set up for display. Forbes kindly reminds everyone that there's no money for movers; besides, he explains, hiring people with no experience in such operations could result in much damage.

John is arguably in over his head as well. Unlike the board members, though, he's relishing it. He immediately enlists the help of Franklin Roosevelt's Works Progress Administration, or WPA, securing in little time two groups of fifty workers, including carpenters, plasterers, and plumbers, along with a crew of eight men dedicated entirely to cleaning. In just sixteen weeks, thanks to 20,000 hours of labor, the old estate has regained much of its former glory.

At this point John puts still another group of WPA workers to the Herculean task of moving and setting up the collections. The library museum alone—a facility that had been open seven days a week since 1904, attracting roughly 75,000 visitors annually—had swelled to include more than 12,000 artifacts. A shortage of display space, however, had left thousands of items packed away in boxes, a great many of them without labels or records of any kind. Day after day, Forbes, along with volunteers Irene Gentry and Emma Cook, work at

In the winter of 1940, twenty-seven-year-old John Ripley Forbes came to the rescue in Kansas City, helping turn the formerly magnificent, but now crumbling Long Mansion into one of the finest natural history museums in the country. Despite facing a staggering amount of renovation and exhibit work, just five months after he arrived the museum opened its doors. Over the next twelve months the Kansas City Museum would attract more than 90,000 visitors, from every state in the nation.

carefully unwrapping the treasures. There are Chinese daggers and ship's models, not to mention a pair of curious-looking perpetual motion machines. There are coins and insects and birds. There are children's dresses from regional Indian tribes, four-barreled pistols—even an old rope, saddle, and trunk from a traveler to the California goldfields in 1849. John transports especially valuable items to the Long Mansion on his own, nesting them in the back seat of his Ford.

Two weeks later, another 140,000 items arrive—some from the historical society, others from private collections. These treasures include fragile bird eggs, the 800-pound head of a whale, buffalo and elephant tusks, a giant fish, and a couple of alligators. From the private collection of Dr. Richard Sutton arrive warrior headdresses and costumes from Bali, ancient spears from the South Seas, and mighty mounted beasts from India and Africa. Incredibly, in the course of all this moving, not a single item or display case is damaged.

The pieces are unpacked and laid out under the high ceilings of the mansion; each piece is inventoried and numbered and its individual history is recorded. Under John's direction, much of the work is accomplished with the help of science and history students from nearby schools. As work progresses, John pauses long enough to introduce the students to a simple cataloging system. The Zoological Department, he explains, which includes Ornithology and Herpetology, will each have an assigned color of card in the catalog file—for example, he instructs, "If one wants to examine birds in the Zoological Department, they consult the green file; if they are interested in mammals, they consult an orange file." (It's always a puzzle to the layperson, he'll later confide, how order may be obtained out of chaos.) Meanwhile, John oversees teams of volunteer taxidermists hunched over bird skins, carefully cleaning feathers and remounting them for display. When all is said and done, John Forbes and his crew will move, clean, catalog, and place in displays more than 300,000 artifacts.

By the spring of 1940 museum association president Arthur Archer, so overwhelmed the previous fall, is showing clear signs of being a happy man. He rarely misses a chance to tell the press about the museum's plans, including a scheme to turn the estate's greenhouse into a botanical museum, and the stable into a 300- to 400-seat auditorium and lecture hall. For his part—and with steady encouragement from one of his most carefully cultivated allies, the Kansas City School Board—Forbes uses his moments with the press to explain that society is past the old days of "building a museum merely to recall the dead." Speaking of activities for young visitors in particular, he tells one group of reporters that "we have no desire to stress the word 'study.'" The museum will be of such broad interest that visitors "will come from all sections of Kansas City and its territory—not because of any self-imposed sense of duty, but because our exhibits and program will themselves attract almost everybody."

Convinced of the wisdom of letting locals carry the flag, Forbes seeks out a dream team of bright, capable women, most of them extremely well connected. One of his star players turns out to be a fifty-one-year-old art lover named Mae Reed Porter. Married to an executive with Kansas City Power and Light, Mae fairly exudes civic-mindedness. When John meets her she is serving on the boards of the celebrated Nelson Gallery of Art, Daughters of the American Revolution, American Association of University Women, National League of American Penwomen, and the Girl Scouts Council of Greater Kansas City.

Porter is passionate about the art of the American West, having routinely beat the back rooms of estate sales and undisplayed museum collections searching for forgotten treasures. Two years before Forbes showed up, she and her daughter Jean had made a trek to the Peale Museum in Baltimore, studying journals and various other artifacts from the Lewis and Clark Expedition. During that visit she convinced the staff to let her shuffle through mounds of dusty cardboard boxes in the museum attic, where she found more than

100 sketches of Native Americans by celebrated artist Alfred Jacob Miller, compiled in 1837 and 1838. Thrilled, she negotiated to buy them from the Peale for $800; twenty-five years later they would be appraised at 200 times that amount.

As she busies herself hanging the Alfred Jacob Miller sketches at the Nelson Gallery in Kansas City, Mae also spends hundreds of hours researching the collection. The result is a popular lecture and slide show called "The West That Was," taken from detailed personal notes she hoped would one day become a book. Her chance would come in the early 1940s, when she presented her ideas to prominent historian Bernard DeVoto. DeVoto would take Mae's writings and sketches, add to and fine-tune them a bit, and eventually turn the material into the book *Across the Wide Missouri*, for which Mae would write the foreword. In 1948 the work would receive the Pulitzer Prize for history; three years later, in 1951, Metro Goldwyn Mayer would premiere the film version of the book, starring Clark Gable, at the Lowe's Midland Theater in Kansas City.

It takes little time or effort for Mae to fall in love with the idea of a museum at the Long Mansion. What's more, she proves astonishingly adept at rendering the museum idea compelling to others, many of them with substantial money in their pockets. Almost from day one, Mae is convinced that twenty-seven-year-old John Ripley Forbes is the man to take the museum from dream to reality. And if Forbes now and then manages to irritate a particular museum board member, grating on the person with his supreme confidence, the team behind him—in particular, Mae Porter—quickly makes an end run for the good of the cause.

For John the biggest challenge of the Long Mansion project isn't the cleaning and moving and setting up of displays but instead has to do with a board unfamiliar with using museum collections in

*Just six months after John blew in to Kansas City in 1940, there helping
to create the city's premier natural history museum in a crumbling mansion
overlooking the Mississippi River, kids were swarming in by the hundreds:
enjoying live animal programs, treasure hunts, and on most days, one
of John's favorite teaching tools – the 16mm nature film.*

service of children's education. Most board members assume that
once the boxes are unpacked and the displays are set up, people
will simply come. The idea of creating a schedule of programs is a
complete mystery. Besides handpicking powerful allies to create "kid
buzz" inside the philanthropic community, Forbes will come to rely
heavily on yet another stable of volunteers—again, most of them
women—to carry out a comprehensive teaching program. Thus,
while Mae Porter is talking to her friends at the Nelson Gallery of
Art about the wonderful opportunity for investment in the Long

Mansion, Mrs. Horace Roy Graham is rallying her own group of socialites, employing them to create a voluntary educational arm of the museum known as the Musettes. Trained by Forbes during the summer of 1940, by fall they're up and running mostly on their own, offering an impressive list of activities for schoolkids across the city.

Incredibly, on May 5, 1940—just five months after Forbes rolled into town in his old Ford—the doors of the museum swing open, receiving in that one day more than 4,500 visitors. Clearly, here is a city ready to love its museum. "There is danger today," Rabbi Samuel Mayerberg says in a dedication ceremony. "We may become complacent and smug, revering the trivial and wrecking our better selves. This museum will create a new sense of respect for the more significant values." Bishop Robert Nelson Spenser concurs, declaring that "this house will be used to awaken wonder in our hearts."

With opening day behind them, John launches a summer lecture series, leading off with what is by then a well-honed portrait of his trip to the Arctic with Donald MacMillan, called "Into the Frozen North." This is followed by a children's presentation by Mrs. Sam Roberts called "The Story of Tomo, an African Lad," based on her recent book *White Mother in Africa*.

Most talked about, though, at least among the kids, is a program Forbes calls "Getting Acquainted with Reptiles," which includes a demonstration with live snakes. He also commandeers a limestone conservatory behind the Long Mansion—a beautiful building trimmed in copper, with a red tile floor and long runs of glass windows. There a turtle pond is constructed, along with a series of large cages on stands, placed against the walls. Among the residents that first summer are four baby skunks, a porcupine, snakes, mice, a squirrel, a young cottontail rabbit, and various young birds. "Let us remember the first concern of the museum should be to obtain public interest," John wrote later. "Once we have the public in the museum we should have no trouble holding that interest and directing them to our most valuable and instructive exhibits."

When it came to featuring live creatures, John was building not only on his work in Stamford but also on that of hundreds of naturalists from the early twentieth century who saw animals as critical ambassadors for science and conservation. It was out of just such enthusiasm that Anna Billings Gallup, curator of the nation's first children's museum in Brooklyn, was convinced to go out on a limb in 1902 and create a collection of live animal displays on the surrounding grounds. Early residents included a tree frog named Billy Joe Springer, plucked from a coal shovel in the boiler room of a freighting ship, as well as Muffty, a barred owl found at Lake Champlain in western Vermont. (Muffty proved especially troublesome, escaping his pen one night and, enthused by his newfound freedom, destroying a large number of butterfly exhibit boxes.) Many museum directors thought Gallup crazy. The preferred method of museum-based education, after all, had long been based on sharing the mounts of dead birds, mammals, mollusks, and insects. Forbes himself had done his share of teaching with just such collections. But thanks in large part to Anna Billings Gallup, and also the staff of the Boston Children's Museum, he had a strong preference for something more.

In Kansas City, John took the concept of live animals a step further. In addition to their use in museum and school programs, he also carried them to hospitals and nursing centers, acting on a belief that living creatures brought a much-needed dose of joy and wonder to the sick and downtrodden. As common as the idea is today (indeed it's hard to find a nursing home without a resident cat or dog), at the time John was making his rounds to Old City Hospital and various convalescent homes in Kansas City with porcupines, rabbits, skunks, and raccoons in tow, the practice was embraced almost nowhere in America.

Sharing animals with the sick and the mentally ill had been limited mostly to Europe and Great Britain, building on an idea first sparked in the ninth century in Gheel, Belgium, where rabbits and a handful of other creatures were used to comfort the handicapped. Yet from there we find little record of live animal therapy until 900 years later, at England's York Retreat. There the Quakers created treatments centered on the observation that when patients with compulsive disorders were given the opportunity to care for chickens and rabbits, most experienced a significant increase in their self-control. So successful was the program at York that animal therapy eventually became part and parcel of asylum reform throughout Europe.

For John Ripley Forbes, as for so many great naturalists in the generation before him, live animals pointed to a fundamental aspect of environmental education: the fact that nature is most powerful when presented as an encounter, an experience—as something intriguing enough to strum the full range of our senses.

September 1940. Every Saturday morning at nine o'clock, the massive doors of the Long Mansion swing open and a smartly dressed attendant makes her way down the sidewalk to a set of iron gates at the edge of the yard. Dozens of kids stand ready, cheering her arrival. Once inside, the children approach another Musette, this one flanked by several helpers. Each child is given a small typewritten question, or clue. It might say: "My tail is long, My jaws are wide, My voice is rough, and so's my hide." And so begins a colossal treasure hunt. Some children fan out through the spacious halls toward the bird exhibits, while others head for the animal displays. Each discovery comes with still another clue—most of them written by a WPA worker named Raymond Phipps—leading to everything from 2,000-year-old Incan mummies to a Confederate Army uniform to Egyptian necklaces to buffalo. Taped on the glass display case at the final treasure is a note that reads something like this: "If you've been sharp, with your brain and eyes, go back to the game table, and claim your prize." Claiming a prize means slipping your hand under the lid of a large pirate chest and feeling about for what seems most intriguing, coming back with anything from a seashell to an arrowhead. In the chest too are framed photos of prized museum exhibits; before long, kids are collecting them like baseball cards.

It never failed to amaze John's coworkers how he could engineer Saturday morning treasure hunts, catalog collections, oversee displays, and give programs—all the while generating public involvement and financial support. At the Long Mansion he cultivated close relationships with reporters, social editors, and photographers from the major newspapers—most notably the *Kansas City Star*, which in turn gave a staggering amount of ink to the museum. Then there was his tireless glad-handing at clubs and churches, in many weeks giving more than a dozen lectures, most complete with slide and film presentations. Early on, when the board of trustees' fund-raising efforts were fizzling, it was John who went knocking on doors, gathering $5,000 in an astonishingly short period of time to keep the project moving forward. The following year he managed to personally shake out another $25,000 for the cause. His willingness to sound the bells and beat the bushes allowed the museum not only to keep going but to attract in its first year an amazing 90,000 visitors, from every state in the nation.

For all his success, though, in the back of Forbes' mind lingered old words of caution, first offered in a letter from Albert Gross at Bowdoin. Gross had worried about John's tendency to "talk too much," sometimes offending the egos of the powers that be. (Writing back, Forbes freely admitted the flaw: "Everything I do, I do with enthusiasm and no doubt by way of talking, overdo this. Will watch it.") In Kansas City he'd gone to great lengths to form alliances with powerful board members—explaining his concerns and strategies, and to those sympathetic, providing whatever information they might need to outmaneuver the skeptics. Even so, it was probably inevitable that he'd make the occasional enemy, finding now and then some powerful man of finance or industry who bristled at the blustery confidence shown by the youngster who had blown into town like a rainmaker, and who, to make matters worse, did in fact seem to have the power to make it rain.

In Kansas City, that man was museum board member Howard H. Peters. Peters was indignant at how John had taken charge of museum matters, not to mention more than a little irritated by the lavish attention the young curator was drawing from both the press and the city elite (achieving the latter, of course, without a hint of social pedigree). Furthermore, Forbes' strong push to include live animals was to Peters nothing but a degrading of the museum. Always before when faced with detractors, John either fired up his supporters or simply parted company and went on to other projects. How entrenched he was willing to get depended on the stakes. Many years later John's son, Ripley, explained that while his father was tactful, "he wouldn't give in if there was value in the effort." (Notably, after John had left a particular museum—and all of them eventually had to fly or fail on their own—he was almost always sought out later for advice, or in many cases hired as a consultant, by the same institution. In 1990, when the Long Mansion Museum turned fifty, John was high on the list of honored guests.)

Albert Gross had once calmly told his young protégé that as you begin to make a place in the world, you're bound to be criticized, especially by fellows envious of your success. "When you get as old as I am," said Gross, "you will pay very little attention either to flattery or adverse criticism." Of the two, he continued, the first is the worst: "If adverse criticism is justified it is good to have it so that we mend our ways; if it is not justified it will do you no harm. I have found it best to keep quiet in either case." There was still an enormous amount of work to be done at the Long Mansion. But Howard Peters was on offense, suited up and ready for battle. And in the end John would pack his bags and leave Kansas City a lot sooner than he'd planned. ✎

Sergeant John Ripley Forbes during World War II, holding a nature class in Alabama. Forbes thought community nature museums were an important part of the war effort at home. "A youth with a well developed sense of compassion for every living thing," he suggested, would be an important ingredient for building American society after victory was achieved.

Chapter Five

THE PEACEFUL WARRIOR

JUST WHEN THINGS WERE GOING MAGNIFICENTLY in Kansas City—the stature of the new museum growing with every passing month—in the spring of 1941 Uncle Sam came looking for John Ripley Forbes. With war raging in Europe, Forbes had the previous February applied for and received confirmation from the draft board of his status as a conscientious objector—an outgrowth of his long membership with the Episcopal Pacifist fellowship. As those who knew him best put it, being a conscientious objector was for John a natural stand to take in light of his deep respect for life in general. To this day no one can recall having seen him kill anything, from a frog to a snake, reflecting his deeply held belief that every creature makes an important contribution to the world. (That said, Forbes did benefit from the harvesting of bird skins in the Arctic by his colleagues, most of which he later placed in natural history museums throughout the Northeast.) Later in life, as a father, John was troubled by the sheer amount of violence being offered as entertainment, for a time refusing to let his son, Ripley, or daughter, Anne, watch war movies on television.

Yet with patriotic feelings running high, and with his brother Fred already suited up for war, John was pressed to explain his position even to members of his family. In a letter to his mother and father two weeks after the attack on Pearl Harbor, he acknowledged that "my stand and the stand of other pacifists is an ideal, but certainly not practical. I am broad enough in my attitude to see the dire need of this nation making an all out effort in this total war; we have been attacked and must fight back." He goes on to assure his parents that he admires his brother Fred, along with all the others who desire to get into the armed forces, offering "tribute to those who so bravely have already given their lives in our country's service. I stand ready to do all in my power for the nation along constructive lines and would like nothing better than to be placed in a position under fire to do this type of work. I have volunteered for such service which might be in the ambulance unit, social service work, civilian defense and a hundred and one other activities necessary to support our armed forces." He continued:

> While I am shocked and outraged at the Pearl Harbor attack, I cannot join the hysterical mass attack on all [Japanese], Germans, Italians and other people on the face of the earth who happen to be on the other side. I cannot hate people of another race just because their leaders have gone mad with lust for power and upset the peace of the entire world. I shall do all in my power to aid this effort short of actual participation in military action from a personal angle. I do it only

because it is the less evil of various courses. I do it because I am an American and proud of this nation.

Forbes would also struggle to explain himself to ardent supporters in Kansas City, assuring them that he was "in no way affiliated with the extremists under the general classification of conscientious objectors." In the event of conflict, he explained to the *Kansas City Star*, "I wish to serve my country as the Quakers did in the last war, doing ambulance and rehabilitation work." One of his biggest supporters in Kansas City, the brilliant Dr. R. L. Sutton, found defending the young curator rankled his own sense of patriotism. "I'll put the cards on the table," he told the Selective Service Board during a hearing about granting John a temporary deferment, his voice shaking with emotion. "To me a conscientious objector is the same as a red rag to a bull. I feel he's a fool and I'd like to kick the pants off him." Still, Sutton made it clear that Forbes was invaluable to the museum effort in Kansas City. "To us he is the museum. He's built this thing on a shoestring. He works like a horse. I've never met a man so fit for the work." Whatever their initial reluctance to bring Forbes on board at the Kansas City Museum, fully two-thirds of the board considered his induction devastating. In fact, so essential did they consider John to daily operations that with his pending departure they called a meeting, struggling to decide whether to attempt to replace him or to simply close the museum for the duration of the war.

Of the almost 12 million men drafted by Selective Service during World War II, about 72,000 filed to be exempted as conscientious objectors. Each faced three options: Those who simply refused to submit to the Selective Service Act ended up in prison. Others went ahead and registered but then worked to be assigned to noncombatant service, often serving with distinction in the medical corps. The third option—the one John chose—was to participate in something known as Civilian Public Service. The administration of CPS fell in part to the so-called historic peace churches, which at the time included the Quakers, the Mennonites, and the Church of the Brethren.

John's orders were to report on June 22, 1941, to a work camp for conscientious objectors located in Magnolia, Arkansas. In a desperate move, a special committee of the Kansas City Museum Association requested an appearance before the ninth ward of the Selective Service Board, pleading for a six-month deferment for their twenty-seven-year-old savior. Mr. Forbes was doing a splendid job, explained representative Mae Porter. Furthermore, he was neck deep in the very fund-raising campaign essential to the continued operation of the museum. Mae stated: "We think his work comes under the line of educational services and that it is essential that he continue."

The bad news, and it was very bad, was that the chairman of the draft board was none other than Forbes' nemesis at the Kansas City Museum, Howard Peters. Peters wasted no time deriding John for his conscientious objector status, calling the effort to classify him as critical to museum education a smoke screen to avoid going to war. Clearly, Peters argued, the "museum would be better off without Forbes." So agitated did Peters become that at one point he announced he was "ready to quit" the draft board if Forbes wasn't sent to a conscientious objector camp in short order. Notably, Forbes' roommate, a Quaker, had asked for and received from the same draft board a four-month deferment to get his business affairs in order.

Meanwhile, bad publicity around John's conscientious objector status continued to mount. On learning that John planned to spend his summer teaching nature studies to children, the Jackson County council of the Veterans of Foreign Wars pushed the panic button, strongly opposing the request for deferment. "We hereby petition the proper authorities to investigate . . . and take necessary steps to stop the spreading of conscientious objector's ideas to the youth of the nation." Outrageous as such comments were, Forbes sought to stem the fallout by choosing to resign his job as supervisor of the Kansas City Museum. "I deem it wise," he explained in his resignation letter, "to resign in order that the board may not be embarrassed by my personal stand."

In a letter to his mother on October 15, 1942, John reflected on his departure from the museum—the second quick exit, if you count his resignation from Stamford in 1937. He wrote:

> Remember my old policy which I have believed in firmly all my life. With proper faith I feel things happen for the best and in cases where it does not happen for the best, with proper courage and faith it can always be turned into the best. Often when things look very black it is the start of something much better. For example the Stamford Museum loss resulted in the [Arctic] Expedition which opened up a future for me far superior to anything I could have ever had had I remained there. While it is still early to see the benefits I firmly believe my loss in Kansas City to the draft has given me something which will benefit me the rest of my life, and open up after the war is over a future beyond anything I could dream of.

Throughout all this turmoil John was trying without success to change his conscientious objector status, which channeled him into the Civilian Public Service, wanting instead to be brought into the military as a "conscientious objector available for noncombatant military service." This alternative military status (known as Class 1 AO), he'd learn too late, was actually necessary in order to be granted temporary deferment. John later said he thought such changes could be made at any time. But sadly, he missed the fine print, which said this sort of reclassification was possible for only five days after original registration. Sure enough, in September 1941 his original status as a conscientious objector was reaffirmed by the Justice Department.

With the writing on the wall, he inquired about applying to a forestry camp in San Dimas, California, thinking the work being done there might be more in line with his current skills. His request was vehemently rejected by L. W. Adamson, one of Howard Peters's close allies on the draft board. Throwing a tantrum of his own, Adamson too threatened to quit the draft board if Forbes was allowed to go to California. "If he is permitted to pick out a camp in California," Adamson sputtered, painting John as a man simply trying to get away with something, "why hasn't every other inducted man a right to pick one in Florida for the winter?" In the end Peters and Adamson prevailed, and Forbes was ordered to report to Arkansas on October 9. The matter finally settled, John showed no inclination to cry over spilled milk. "I'm ready to go," he told a reporter for the *Kansas City Star*, "and have been for the last month."

Camps established by Civilian Public Service for conscientious objectors were to have both a staff person representing the sponsoring church (the camp Forbes was sent to was sponsored by the Quakers) as well as a project supervisor, there to oversee the interests of the federal government. These two supervisors, working with the camp director, were charged with devising lists of specific duties and responsibilities for each of the men stationed there. The government pushed hard for the men to take on jobs in service of the actual war. The peace churches, on the other hand, were in favor of their working outside the war effort per se while still performing tasks important to the nation as a whole. It was a disagreement that never went away.

Conscripts to Civilian Public Service were not only not paid by the government, but had to come up with $35 a month toward their housing and food. Though Forbes was sponsored by the Quakers, other churches, including his own Episcopal Pacifist Fellowship, helped raise the monthly payments for their members. Finally, there was to be no compensation for any accidents the men might suffer, nor any dependency benefits.

In a few places, instead of uniforms the men were given overalls with a broad stripe painted down the front and the back, making them easy marks for disapproving people in nearby communities. At several facilities, including Camp Germfask in northern Michigan, locals coming across groups of conscientious objectors detained them, then beat them senseless. Now and then young girls ran up to the lines of men standing at attention and inserted chicken feathers into their buttonholes. Eager to feed the rising tide of patriotism, the press piled on. Popular national magazines passed along all manner of unsubstantiated rumors, including one that said conscientious objectors were routinely sneaking out of the camps and impregnating local girls.

What would draw conscientious objectors squarely into the spotlight, however, was an endless stream of media attacks against the wildly popular movie star Lew Ayres, a long-standing pacifist. Ayres had starred opposite Greta Garbo in the 1929 movie *The Kiss*, went on to full-blown stardom in 1930 with *All Quiet on the Western*

Front, and then settled into full-time heartthrob status in 1938 when he starred in the first of several *Dr. Kildare* films. That such a popular public figure should reveal himself a conscientious objector in the face of a world war was in the military's eyes bad press of spectacular proportions. In theaters across the country, Ayres's movies were canceled, sometimes under threat of violence. The Boston City Council instructed the community censor to revoke the business license of any theater that dared show one of his films.

Among Ayres's few defenders, none was more steadfast than Hollywood radio and print columnist Hedda Hopper. Hopper wrote: "Twelve years ago the world was acclaiming this same lad when he was an unknown actor because he carried a great message against war in 'All Quiet on the Western Front.' Now they stand ready to crucify him because he is still against war." Ayres could have easily gotten himself one of the lush spots in the Army, argued Hopper, as so many others in Hollywood had done. "There are many in this town crying out against him as they lean back in their swivel chairs and adjust the trousers of their brand new uniforms to keep the creases in. I say Lew has much more courage than they." A lone round of follow-up defense came by way of a column in the *New York Times* titled "The Case of Lew Ayres." If all humanity believed what Ayres believed, the writer suggested—a creed that turned on nonresistance to evil—there would be no Nazis and no war. The essayist wrote: "A minute handful of Americans do believe this creed. We have no reason to hope, from what we know of the human mind and emotions that the whole world will accept it in any time we can foresee. But let us not on that account hold back an honest tribute to a man who gives up a rich career and faces public ridicule and contempt because he will not hide the faith that is in him."

John, meanwhile, on many days was less than happy with the

Civilian Public Service. He resented inductees who were unwilling to work, as well as camp leaders who in the face of such problems could only manage to wring their hands in dismay. Writing in the *Conscientious Objector* in the spring of 1942, Forbes warned that such weaknesses would lead to a further loss of goodwill in local communities, which in turn could threaten the entire program. To get errant boys on the right path, he suggested—sounding rather like a camp counselor—will take both patience and correction. He believed all new conscientious objectors, and also those in need of a little rehabilitation, should be sent first to an induction camp for intensive training, preferably in a facility located away from local communities. Only on the recommendation of the induction camp director should the men then be sent on to the regular camps. Those who failed at such induction centers, Forbes proposed, should be sent back to their draft boards, where they would face a choice of either going to jail or being reclassified to active duty. While the editors of the *Conscientious Objector* thought well of John's idea of induction training centers, they took strong exception to the notion of sending those who couldn't conform back to their draft boards. "The whole basis of the pacifist philosophy," wrote editor Jay Nelson Tuck, "is that no government has the right to force any man into military service over his conscientious scruples. If a man be a sincere conscientious objector, we have no right on earth to deny him exemption from the business of war, just as we deny that the government or any other power has that right."

After six frustrating months at two different CO camps, Forbes petitioned yet again for a change in his status, to Class 1 AO (conscientious objector available for noncombatant military service), requesting immediate induction into the United States Army. "I believe in the ideals of the absolute pacifist," he said in a written statement to the Associated Press on May 10, 1942, "but no longer feel it is possible to put such ideals into effect. I wish to aid the war effort and have decided my choice lies between two evils, one of which I must choose." The men who remained behind in the camps, he insisted, "deserve and merit our respect. If we are the tolerant democracy which we claim, we must allow the government and peace churches to carry on." John saw his position as an absolute pacifist at one end of the scale, with combat soldiering on the other end. "I cannot take either position and have come to the realization that I must compromise and take a middle of the road course." Rather than a conscientious objector, he explained, he would from now on be a "Conscientious Co-operator."

If that seems like a retreat, it's worth noting that Forbes continued to push hard for the road of peace, gently chastising a society willing to fight for tolerance overseas while being incapable of protecting it within its own borders. While we may not agree with their actions, he wrote in a long unpublished essay called "To Victory with Tolerance," "to do anything which would destroy them or what they stand for is cutting the very heart out of our great democratic way of life, the very principle for which we are fighting." Throw these young men into jail, into concentration camps, or condemn them to death, he chided, "but don't expect our young soldiers to be fighting for our present great ideals. Like Germany and the axis, we'll at that point instead be reduced to fighting for selfish political reasons, for territory."

Many of us, he continued—"with much thought, prayer and meditation—have left our jail cells, our camps, and civilian life to go directly into the army in non combatant service. We hope that we alongside the soldier and statesman may bring to a war weary world a lasting peace."

While serving in the Army during World War II, mostly in the rural South, John Ripley Forbes never missed a chance to create nature study opportunities for kids. Here a group of students from Geneva County, Alabama set out to explore the world of butterflies.

Over the next twelve months, during his off hours at an Army Air Force detachment at Napier Field in Dothan, Alabama, Forbes would attempt to publish "To Victory with Tolerance" in fifteen different national magazines, from *Reader's Digest* to *Christian Century*, with no success. Some editors thought the topic had already received enough coverage, mostly through the verbal volleys that followed the Lew Ayres story. Still others sympathized with John's views but feared a strong backlash from advertisers.

If writing on the topic of conscientious objectors proved a hard sell, John managed to land a fair amount of ink in service of other opinions, mostly linking the objectives of the war to guiding principles of education. To his way of thinking, the two came together nowhere better than in the community nature museum. "Keeping alive the sensitivity of children to love and respect the individuality of life is an important task facing every educational institution," he wrote in a 1942 article for *National Humane Review*. "A youth that has a well developed sense of compassion for every living thing, is a necessary factor in the building of the new social order after final victory has been achieved."

The time had come, he offered, to channel the nation's overwhelming emotions about war into a commitment to the welfare of future generations. In the midst of such darkness it fell to museums to fill the minds of young people with wholesome ideas, with ideals of tolerance, kindness, and love of races beyond creed or color. "Ours is a grave responsibility," he told his fellow curators. "Unless such ideals are kept alive, our soldiers will have given their lives in vain. The children must be saved to take the leadership in a better world of the future, a future in which we their fathers and

May the beauty of the Christmas season bring strength and courage to a troubled world. As our armed forces strive to bring about a world where PEACE will again be universal, may I ask you to dedicate yourself this Christmas season to the welfare of our children.

Force, hate, brutality and torture must not be a part of their lives. We must direct their minds to channels that will keep foremost in their thoughts the ideals of kindness, understanding, justice and love.

John Ripley Forbes

Though a pacifist all his life, soldier John Ripley Forbes saw World War II as an opportunity to reinvigorate America's most cherished values. This holiday greeting is from 1945.

brothers are giving our lives to make possible." Given the enormous weight civic leaders were by then placing on museums, having finally learned to see them as critical adjuncts to public schools, it was a message that fell on friendly ears.

Similar ideas had actually arisen in the early 1900s, when large numbers of immigrants were arriving in America. Museums, said leaders of that earlier day, would play a critical role in easing radical tendencies in foreigners, primarily by giving them a proper set of stories with which to navigate their new country. For many in the 1940s, then, it wasn't that big of a stretch to think of the values and ideals Americans were dying for in Europe and Japan as properly being enshrined in museums. What was unique about Forbes' argument—a kind of John Dewey perspective fortified by America's love affair with nature and science—was to claim natural history as a key element in such society building. Plain and simple, nature fostered interest and intrigue in young people. And that interest would in turn lead to a strong, confident populace—to a nation more scientifically savvy, to be sure, but also one with enough imagination to think outside the box, to find a way forward through the tumult of a rapidly changing world.

On arriving at Alabama's Napier Field, Forbes was assigned jobs as both librarian and assistant special service officer, charged with overseeing recreation and education opportunities for the soldiers. He wasted no time jumping on the Victory Book Campaign, sponsored by the American Library Association, the United Service Organizations (USO), and the American Red Cross. Despite a long string of Army paperwork jams, he managed not only to secure a new building with furniture but to raise $3,000 for additional books and to hire an experienced civilian librarian. Under his direction, the Post Library at Napier Air Field became a model for much of the eastern half of the country, with some 9,000 volumes in circulation. Furthermore, the books he acquired landed not only in the main library but also on carts in the hospital, in the chapel, and ultimately in fourteen other branch collections. Forbes exclaimed: "You can't expect a husky young soldier headed for combat duty to take a feverish interest in the State Papers of Grover Cleveland, the 'Ladies Guide to Home Needlework,' or a dog-eared arithmetic of the vintage of 1904!" With that success under his belt, he set about preparing to do something similar in his next position at nearby Moody Field, gaining a $5,000 book appropriation even before his transfer papers were signed.

During his off time (if such a thing can even be imagined for John), in the fall of 1942 he made an ambitious expansion of his "Hornaday Fund," created earlier in honor of his old friend and mentor, by turning it into the William T. Hornaday Foundation. The new foundation's goals were hardly modest. It would set up children's museums in various industrial cities in the eastern half of the United States, paying as much attention as possible to the poor and disenfranchised. Although one could imagine that serving in the Army might be a barrier to such lofty ambitions, that wasn't the case. Having first assembled an administrative board for the foundation, John began volunteering on his days off in southern Alabama's impoverished Geneva County, which at the time suffered from one of the highest illiteracy rates in the nation.

He made nature presentations at dozens of schools and libraries. In the little town of Slocumb he established the first children's museum for black students in America. Next, he set about rounding up endorsements from the local school board to establish a traveling nature program, designed to reach poorer kids, including the black populations, who without transportation had little chance to visit an actual brick-and-mortar museum.

Within the month he'd gathered duplicates and cast-off artifacts from major museums from New England to California, acquiring everything from Hopi Indian art to boxes of minerals, insects, and butterflies; mounted birds and bird eggs, more than 500 jigsaw puzzles, and a mounted skunk, woodchuck, and muskrat. Many of the exhibits he'd been collecting found a home in a large room located in the basement of the Geneva Library. Soon the little museum had displays from the Field Museum in Chicago, the Brooklyn Children's Museum, the Denver Art Museum, the Indianapolis Children's Museum, and Michigan's Cranbrook Museum of Science. One of John's most steadfast suppliers of display objects would be the American Museum of Natural History in New York, where his good friend James Clark was always at the ready to secure treasures for him, plucking them from extras held in the museum vaults.

As the workload in Alabama grew, John hired as both field representative for the Hornaday Foundation and curator of the new Geneva County Nature Museum a twenty-four-year-old single woman from Denver named Ada Neville, paying her an annual salary of $2,000. Shortly after graduating from high school, Neville had worked at the Denver Museum's "Golden Gate International Exhibition," preparing and managing the Federal Building Indian exhibit, followed by stints at a children's theater. She was bright, self-motivated, and a big believer in the Hornaday mission. Although her experience with children's museums was limited, together she and Forbes were a potent whirlwind. "We have a great opportunity and can do a world of good," John told Ada early on. Ada heartily agreed.

As Ada Neville traveled back and forth across Geneva County, children spotting her car winding up the dirt road to the schoolhouse would announce her arrival with loud cries of "The museum is coming!" A gaggle of eager kids would immediately pour out of the school to begin carrying into the classroom films and projector, exhibit boxes, and most notably, cages with live animals for the weekly museum hour. After finishing there, Ada might motor off another ten or fifteen miles, this time to meet up with a crowd of eager black children in another part of the county. Because most black schools had no electricity available to power a film projector, the kids often gathered instead in a nearby church, where they might watch a show about birds, or find out how many caterpillars a cuckoo could eat, or—and this would've been particularly relevant to the children of sharecroppers—discover what birds fed on tomato worms and boll weevils. Through it all, John and Ada took pains to tailor their presentations to the teachers' existing lesson plans. A class already studying reptiles, for example, could expect Ada to show up with the movie *Getting Acquainted with Reptiles*, along with a live bull snake to be passed around to anyone who wanted to hold it. One class had been watching a pair of beavers at work erecting a dam near the schoolhouse, so Ada returned the following week with a mounted beaver as well as a film showing baby beavers in their underwater home—a sight that, as Forbes later described it, brought down the house.

Still, the rural South of the 1940s was a cautious place, guided by long-standing social protocols of which neither John nor Ada had any knowledge. Keeping his commitment to serve the disadvantaged, Forbes made a special point of sending traveling shows to the

During his time in the Army John used furlough time to set up nature programming for hundreds of children in the rural South. On being told that black and white kids were forbidden to mix, he simply created museums for each group. If a school didn't have the electricity he needed to show nature films – and this was often the case in black schools – he moved the program to a nearby church.

poorest children, including those of black sharecroppers living in the area. While planning a nature film show in the spring of 1944, Ada Neville was surprised to receive a letter from the owner of the Royal and Friendly theaters in Samson and Slocomb, Alabama, lining out strict terms for the upcoming program.

Since talking with you on the phone recently concerning the free shows for school children to be held at Samson and Slocomb, I must make the following restrictions in both places:

I cannot open the main auditorium to Colored pupils due to the fact that some of my patrons object.

We held a show for Colored school pupils at Slocomb some time ago in the main auditorium and my manager tells me that a few of the white people took offense at this and had not been back to the theater since. So I do not wish to deviate from the customs and practices set by our people to the extent that it would hurt my business.

You are welcome to invite the Colored pupils to be present in the balcony of the theater at the same time you show to white pupils or you may have a separate show if you use the balcony only for colored. I can take care of about 40 in the balcony of each house.

Yours very truly.
W.P. Pato

Such problems aside, as far as Forbes and his new assistant could tell, things could hardly be going any better. Superintendent of Education J. J. Collins seemed thrilled with John Forbes and Ada Neville, declaring Ada to be "most marvelous . . . an excellent instructor, devoted worker, good mixer and ideal in every respect."

The accolades rolled in for several months; then suddenly, in July, Collins wanted nothing more to do with Ada Neville. He instructed her to abandon all efforts in service of the Geneva Museum and to seek work elsewhere. Though it took John weeks to unravel the story, in the end he learned the sour mood was the result of Collins having discovered that—on her own time, away from the job and in a private home—Ada had had the gall to smoke cigarettes and drink alcohol. Trying to sound a voice of reason, the president of the museum association told Collins that Ada was doing an excellent job. "I frankly don't think she has done anything," the president wrote in a letter to Forbes. "And if Mr. Collins fired all of his teachers that smoke or drank he would be short some teachers."

Forbes, himself neither a smoker nor a drinker, wasted no time writing a letter to the Geneva County Children's Museum Association, deploring this treatment of a committed worker. Admonished Forbes: "If Mr. Collins and whoever has complained to him about our curator smoking want to put this issue above so vital a project as the Children's Museum, then they can be prepared to take full blame for its failure. And the community's many children, who have benefited by such a program and were looking forward to the coming school years with new interest, may look to their Superintendent of Schools and those who have criticized Miss Neville as being to blame for bringing this vital work to an end." Collins, meanwhile, had plenty of friends willing to fuel "a war," as Ada came to call it, "between the carousers versus the uplifts." Shortly before she left the Geneva County project, someone tipped off an FBI agent by the name of Miller that she'd been making suspicious trips to the nearby town of Rucker. Word on the street was that she'd been gathering military secrets from the soldiers and passing them to unknown enemies. Miller investigated, interviewing several community members. He discovered Ada's trips to Rucker were to borrow films from an Army visual aids library, part of her work for the Hornaday Foundation.

"Girl, you really made a hit in that town," Forbes joked in a letter to Ada some months after she left Alabama.

"I feel quite important," she replied from her new job at the Denver Art Museum. "Nobody is anybody until they have been investigated by the FBI, and I feel I've made the ranks of something or other."

As one of the Geneva museum board members later put it to John, "Personally I am very fond of Ms. Neville, but of course Mr. Collins could never be reconciled to her modern warp in this old fashioned Southern county."

If Ada's smoking, drinking, and alleged spying weren't enough to reinforce fear of outsiders in Geneva, an article in the April 1945 issue of *Life* magazine showing a uniformed Sergeant John Ripley Forbes talking to a circle of eager schoolboys was more than enough to do the job. Editors at the magazine, having heard of a young soldier establishing nature museums in rural Alabama, found it just the kind of human interest story *Life* was famous for. Unfortunately, their city ways were showing. The aforementioned picture of Forbes with schoolkids showed the boys kneeling; being summer, those with their backs to the camera could be seen not wearing shoes. The caption referred to Geneva, Alabama, "where most of the children wear bare feet." The article went on to describe the nature films Forbes was showing as a special treat for the children, since "most have never seen a movie before."

They might as well have blown their noses on the Alabama flag. Geneva residents were livid—some claiming Forbes set up the slam through the Hornaday Foundation to get back at them for the bad treatment of Ada Neville. "Everybody is up in arms over the *Life* pictures and mostly what was said," wrote museum association president Mrs. Joel Johnson. "I have been cussed and discussed and bawled out and blamed for this from all over the county. Mrs. Stutts called me and asked that I call a meeting and dissolve our relationship with the Hornaday Foundation. Our museum project is dead. We will never be able to do a thing with it." Then, the following day, another letter from Mrs. Johnson: "The committee appreciates the fact that you damn Yankees want to help the South, but we sure don't need that kind of help. Forbes you will have to learn things like this can't be done; let it be a lesson to you if you work among the Southern people anymore."

Though many residents of Geneva had been thrilled to have *Life* magazine in their midst, they felt betrayed. The most severe reaction erupted from H. G. Wilkinson, owner and editor of the aptly named *Geneva County Reaper*, who seemed to have only slightly less contempt for Forbes than he did for the now failing Adolf Hitler. The entire article in "their vile rag," he wrote, "is a confounded lie, a barefaced falsehood. It will be seen that the youngsters in the foreground in overalls were caused to kneel [Forbes was eventually blamed for this, as well], so that the bottoms of their [dirty] bare feet were exposed to the all seeing eye of the camera." Citing copyright laws that prohibited him quoting the magazine exactly, he assured his readers that the words were "well chosen to accomplish their end—to hold the South up before the world as a cesspool of ignorance, backwardness, rags and dirty bare feet." As for Forbes and his so-called nature programs, "any of these kids could have taken this ornamental sergeant two miles from town and lost him so completely he would have never found his way back." Stuffed skunks, ducks, and snakes, wrote Wilkinson, "may be a novelty to the youngsters here. We don't have to stuff the darn things—we grow them natural-like down here, and our youngsters know all about them. In short, *Life Magazine*, your story of Geneva county youth is a damn lie, and there is not a word of truth in it."

Though in fact John had warned the community ahead of time that he had no control over what *Life* printed, no amount of apology, no number of requests to the magazine to print a correction, could ever put him back on good footing. He made several offers to continue supplying the museum with display items from his own collections, outside the Hornaday Foundation, just to keep the kids on board, but to no avail. As board member Mrs. Stutts put it: "The *Life* pictures have made such a wave of indignation that it will take fifty years to get over it."

Twelve months earlier John had been described in the *Montgomery [Alabama] Advertiser* as a tireless champion of education, who "spent every spare moment away from Army duty . . . covering a 140-mile area." With Ada Neville's help, he was reaching some 14,000 students—not only teaching but also combating juvenile delinquency. "It is safe to say," the editor of the *Advertiser* proclaimed, that "[the children of south Alabama] will remember Sergeant John Ripley Forbes," who "brought with him a gift that children never forget—an understanding of the inhabitants of nature's world."

But in the blink of an eye Forbes had become just another damn Yankee. After the smoke cleared and the museum was history, Mrs. Johnson said she had never seen such disappointment "in children all over the county." In time the museum effort would again gain a faint breath of life, moving into a spare room in a school building. This time, though, it would be confined to showing films on-site and displaying a small handful of exhibits.

It's worth noting that not every southern community felt slighted by the *Life* story. Indeed, the Hornaday Foundation received inquiries from people in towns across the South asking how to set up similar programs of their own. At least one new Hornaday project, a children's museum in Wilsonville, Alabama, was a direct result of the article.

Whether it was a source of relief or consternation is hard to say, but by the time the *Life* article hit the stands, John had been transferred out of Geneva to serve as education and recreation leader for the Maxwell Field Convalescent and Rehabilitation Center near Montgomery. When not writing long letters of apology to the folks in Geneva, he again threw himself into Army work. No sooner had he settled in before he called a meeting of officers to describe what he considered necessary steps to create a successful convalescent program. The most important thing, he explained, is to know your men intimately. Since it was impossible in a convalescent center the size of those being run by the Army to pull off that kind of intimacy, the trick (much like using women's groups in museums) was to employ as helpers those convalescing patients who showed a special interest in the work.

The second cornerstone, John continued, involved instilling confidence in the patient about the program. This could be achieved only by being more interested in what the men needed and wanted than in one's own simple charge to invest a certain number of hours into the task (far too many of which, he believed, went into filling out Special Service reports). Forbes argued that the men would have confidence in the program at the point it deserved their support. "Deal your cards from the top," he advised. "Don't insult the soldiers by building up a party for them that you know full well isn't going to measure up to the sales talk."

The third and final "must," John explained, was one he himself had by then perfected to a remarkable degree: sell yourself. If the men believe in you and your program, John advised, your activities will be a howling success. Refuse politely those things you know won't be well received. John elaborated: "Let me give you an example of an incident that took place last week. We were called by a local minister, who asked if we would get a group of convalescents to come to his church to attend the morning service and enjoy a chicken dinner by his young people to be followed by a late afternoon service. I do not need to tell you men that a party with strings attached is not very welcomed. To expect the men to attend church twice would naturally have killed any interest in the affair."

The world in the spring of 1944 remained a place of great tension and chaos. The Anzio campaign, designed to breathe new life into the Allied effort to capture Rome, was bogged down, suffering heavy casualties. Alfred Rosenberg, Germany's Reich Minister for the Eastern Occupied Territories, carried out a heartbreaking plan to kidnap 40,000 Polish children and use them as slave laborers. Toward the end of summer Anne Frank and her family would be arrested by the Gestapo in Amsterdam. And the liberation of the first concentration camps by Russian troops was still months away.

Against this troubling backdrop John Forbes was starting his next assignment at the Army Air Force's convalescent hospital at Gunter Field in Nashville, Tennessee. He was shocked by what he found there. With his encouragement, in May 1944 a team of five officers assigned to the center wrote to Lieutenant Colonel Howard Rusk, pleading for patients who they said were in states of apathy and despair. "Because of the unfortunate conditions which they have been forced to accept," the officers wrote, "the patient morale is so low that we fear many of them will go AWOL within a week unless steps are immediately taken to correct the present trouble."

Much of the problem centered on hospital surgeon Lieutenant Colonel Egan, who had decided it was best to direct the rehabilitation program with an iron fist. Among other things, Egan was fond of telling patients he would make their hospital stay so tough they'd be begging to return to overseas duty. Patients barely a minute late for meetings or other assignments were considered AWOL, subject to a term in the guardhouse. As for any severely wounded or otherwise traumatized soldier who applied for disability compensation, the person was "not fit to be a citizen of the United States."

Later that year, a small photo appeared in *Time* magazine under the heading "Hospital for Heroes?" decrying deplorable conditions at Christie Street Health Center in Toronto. Soon afterward, again with encouragement from Forbes, a small group of convalescing soldiers in Nashville wrote a letter to *Time*'s editor, hoping for similar exposure. "We found ourselves quartered in tar-papered barracks which had already been considered completely unfit by a general of the Army Medical Corps," the letter began. Latrines and washrooms were located far from the barracks, forcing such long walks for patients that in winter months they often suffered from exposure. In summer, meanwhile, heat-stricken soldiers could routinely be seen vomiting behind their barracks.

Located beside a railroad switching yard in a seedy pocket of industrial Nashville, each of the barracks was heated by a coughing coal stove. Upper respiratory infections, ranging from bronchitis to pneumonia, were higher there than at any other installation in the country. Ironically, Forbes noted, German prisoners of war were living nearby at Camp Forrest, about seventy miles from Nashville, in comfortable barracks with central heating and washrooms.

◈

When not battling the bureaucracy, on his days off John kept the Hornaday Foundation rolling—most notably, helping a group of locals establish the Nashville Children's Museum, destined to become one of the finest in the nation. Besides being the "source of inspiration," as museum association president Vernon Sharp called him, Forbes found himself again the early point man for fund-raising, securing the project's full $15,000 budget in just under twenty weeks. Once a building was found, he once again started calling on curator friends from around the country for exhibit loans, at one point grabbing a three-day pass from the Army on a quest for specimens. Riding to the rescue was the ever-faithful James Clark at the American Museum of Natural History, who sent three large vans of display items, including a splendid set of large mammal mounts. At the Smithsonian, John managed to procure several hundred pounds more, including two enormous coyotes from 1884, taken in the field and prepared by none other than William Hornaday.

The Nashville museum effort was blessed with key players ready for action from the start—from the superintendent of schools to Vanderbilt University chancellor O. C. Carmichael. "Children's museums will supply the thing that we have not had in our educational system before," Carmichael assured the public, "and are worthy of very genuine and enthusiastic support." Staying true to John's original ideal, that such nature museums were especially important for disadvantaged kids, the association decided to locate their museum in a three-story, twenty-five-room stone building—

During his last months in the Army John helped establish the Cumberland Museum in Nashville, Tennessee. Staying true to his ideal of bringing nature to disadvantaged kids, the effort began with the renovation of a broken down three-story stone building in one of the poorest sections of the city. The Museum was later renamed the Cumberland Museum and Science Center, and in 1974 was moved to a new facility.

crumbling, with not a single pane of glass intact—in one of the poorest sections of the city. After being discharged from the Army in the autumn of 1945, Forbes came on for a time as acting director, helping to grow the operation to include a junior museum staff comprised of local high school science students, more than a dozen volunteer curators, and yet another powerful women's division, this one headed by Mrs. Rufus Fort.

Thanks to the fierce dedication of its founders, programming at the Nashville museum grew faster than a ditch full of chickweed. There were class tours and talks at schools, as well as what was fast becoming a Forbes staple—regular visits, often with live animals, to hospitals as well as to a local school for the blind. An array of after-school clubs began meeting at the museum, focusing on everything from history and art to nature study and gardening. By 1948, the Nashville Children's Museum was serving more than 50,000 children a year.

From Nashville, word spread fast. Soon there came a plea for help from Jacksonville, Florida, written by a fledgling museum group unable to find its wings. John answered the call shortly before being discharged from the Army, needing just twelve days of a two-week furlough to survey the program, organize the board, and hire a director. Shortly after this project came similar requests from Holtville, Alabama, and Durham, North Carolina. Following his discharge Forbes served as midwife for a project in Fort Worth, Texas, where he convinced the city to include a children's wing in an upcoming museum bond issue; two years later, Fort Worth broke ground on a separate $300,000 children's museum. In all these projects, the Hornaday Foundation took the role of consultant—helping organize the board and volunteers; furnishing displays, equipment, and personnel; and providing enough money for locals to hit the ground running. As Temple Fielding of the *Christian Science Monitor* described Hornaday Foundation activities: "When the museum is thoroughly organized, the elders stirred up, and the children practically breaking down the doors to see it, the Foundation moves on."

In his final year before leaving the Army, John wrote a flood of

John Ripley Forbes was passionate about bringing the wonders of nature to disadvantaged kids, whether they were from poor neighborhoods, or sick or handicapped. Here two blind children from Fort Worth, Texas enjoy an encounter with a raccoon.

letters to gain funding for the Hornaday Foundation. One of the biggest fish to bite was Arthur Newton Pack of the American Nature Association, who agreed to a $7,000 gift across two years if John could raise matching funds (which of course he did). The money funded efforts in Fort Worth, Orlando, Durham, Charlotte, and

Atlanta. Another contributor who looked promising was Major Max Fleischmann, a wealthy businessman who had given a large check to fund a museum in Santa Barbara, California. But Fleischmann responded to John's solicitation with a tart letter, describing his push to use live animals as an effort to turn otherwise respectable natural history museums into zoos. John responded right away, patiently arguing that when it came to children, a well-run, humane live animal program was just the spark to set kids off on a lifetime path of learning. Much to John's surprise, Fleischmann yielded, putting in place what would become a modest annual contribution to the Hornaday Foundation.

One of the last places Sergeant Forbes hung his hat before being discharged in the fall of 1945 was Plattsburg, New York. On November 27, immediately prior to leaving the Army, he attended a farewell address to the soldiers by Colonel Lester Crago. Crago told the separatees that war was inevitable—that if these men were not themselves back fighting again in the years to come, they could count on their own children taking their places. Barely had Crago left the podium before John rushed back to the barracks and wrote an angry letter of complaint to Brigadier General Max Schneider, stating in part: "It is certainly not keeping faith with those who have made the supreme sacrifice to infer it was all in vain and we shall have another war directly. I am sure I speak for many of the men when I protest any officer showing so little faith in the ideals for which we fought." Schneider wrote back three weeks later, telling Forbes he'd referred his letter to the commanding officer at Plattsburg for appropriate action.

Pacifist John Ripley Forbes left the Army without looking back. Nestled in his foot locker were the Victory Medal, the Good Conduct Medal, and the American Theater Medal.

Within a few short years of John leaving the Army, the William T. Hornaday Memorial Foundation had helped launch nearly a dozen museums; several, including the Jacksonville Museum in Florida and the Fort Worth Children's Museum, were on their way to becoming among the most admired facilities of their kind in the country. On July 3, 1944, Eleanor Roosevelt highlighted John's work in her hugely popular syndicated column "My Day." "I have seen how much the children enjoy these museums planned for their benefit," she wrote, "and I am sure that this is one of the ways in which we can promote a development of a very healthy interest in nature." Likewise, Roy Chapman Andrews—the adventurous, globe-trotting archaeologist and former director of the American Museum of Natural History— confessed his own admiration for the Hornaday Foundation's efforts. "Certainly there never was a time when work with children was more needed," Andrews said. Approval also came from popular nature writer Thornton Burgess, as well as the New York commissioner of corrections, who began pushing hard for nature museums as a way to stem the rising tide of juvenile delinquency.

Perhaps conservationist Edward Preble best summed up John's work: "One of the earliest enthusiasms of a child is his love for living creatures. With this interest already implanted in the pupil, it is easy, by well-directed effort, to guide his actions along lines that through life will add to his joy, and strengthen his influence for the perpetuation of organisms that have so benefited him. The development of the William T. Hornaday Memorial Foundation . . . seems to me a particular happy project well worthy of generous and widespread support."

But there was no time to rest on such laurels. Plenty of untapped opportunities for kids existed in other states—just waiting to rise, as John later described it, "out of the must, dust, and cobwebs." Across one period of eighteen months, from shortly after his discharge to the fall of 1947, John would travel some 63,000 miles, putting together what by then had grown to more than a million separate artifacts and exhibits. Soon he would be on his way to California. There he would start more nature museums, of course. But he was also about to refine one of the most popular, most controversial ideas in the history of the urban nature movement. ✍

*A class in Kingsburg, California enjoying a deodorized skunk from one of
John's nature museums. Among the earliest animal lending programs had
been one created for the public schools by the Wisconsin Humane Society.
There too, teachers had been hugely enthusiastic. As one described it: "A
month's stay in a classroom by a family of guinea pigs has more effect on the
attitude of children toward animals than any amount of classroom lecture."*

Chapter Six

BORROWING PETUNIA

A child will learn more easily, and learn more,
from one living, moving animal or bird than from
a whole museum full of artfully stuffed corpses.

John Ripley Forbes
National Humane Review, 1954

AUTUMN 1953. Inside the California Junior Museum in Sacramento stands a wobbly line of two dozen kids, talking and giggling and bobbing up and down on the balls of their feet. Second in line is a blond-haired boy named Ricky, biting his lip, nervously rubbing the top of his tennis shoe against the back of his leg, looking very much like he's about to wet his pants. His eyes dart from the man behind the desk, then around the room, as if looking for someone who might be able to make the little girl with pigtails waiting patiently in front of him move a little faster. The object of his desire is in the corner of the room, resting in a carrying cage—a year-old skunk named Petunia. A fifth-grader named Alice, standing right behind Ricky, is also plainly excited, eager to show off a white rat named Harry to her mother's friends at their Saturday afternoon knitting session.

Although John Ripley Forbes had argued vigorously for live animal displays in Kansas City, in California his drive to link kids with critters would rise to new heights. Within a few short years, his "animal lending library" would find its way into the pages of a remarkable array of newspapers and magazines, from the *Saturday Evening Post* to *Reader's Digest*, from *Life* to *Popular Mechanics*. "A child's response to any living thing is emotional," Forbes would later explain in a 1967 article in *Parent's* magazine. "When he is face to face with a real live animal, when his fingers touch a bumpy shell or soft fur, his response is full of feeling."

Much the same idea had driven one of the first animal lending libraries in the nation, run by the Wisconsin Humane Society in Milwaukee. That program, however, which also included chickens, dogs, and cats, involved placing animals directly into the classrooms of the public school system. Milwaukee teachers praised the effort, claiming a month's stay in a classroom by a family of guinea pigs had more effect on the attitude of children toward animals than any amount of classroom lecture. By the 1950s the appeal of that idea had grown even stronger, especially given that kids' attention was by then being increasingly commanded by that new, flickering electronic gadget in the corner of the living room called the television. "Between television and all manner of mechanical inventions," explains John's wife, Margaret, "John came to sense an increasing urgency in the work."

John's animal lending library, officially launched in Sacramento, was carefully regulated. Boys and girls age seven years and older

Creatures in Forbes' animal lending libraries were grouped in tiers, depending on the level of care they required. First division animals could be loaned out to any trained, qualified child. Second division animals were loaned only to kids ten and older with previous experience. A final tier was established for school teachers, scout leaders and older teens who'd demonstrated competence in animal handling.

were trained in the care of small, mostly native mammals, many of which had been injured in the wild or raised in captivity. Instead of merely interacting with these animals in the museum, however—which was standard practice in more progressive museums in the East and Midwest—here kids were permitted to "check out" critters for up to a week. Younger children were allowed to take out only those animals requiring the least amount of care. Adults too were keen on the idea, with elementary teachers showing up regularly to check out animals for their classrooms. Hospital volunteers, meanwhile—often members of the local Junior League—carried possums and skunks and foxes to pediatric wards throughout the city. One day California Junior Museum director Mike Merkel agreed to loan a fox to a minister, who seemed convinced the animal would help his congregation stay awake during Sunday sermons.

Circulating at a rate of between twenty and forty a week, the animals ranged from blackbirds and magpies to rabbits and rats, from hamsters and mice to turtles, lizards, snakes, and porcupines. The fine for overdue critters was ten cents a day. One boy was excused from the fine when the rat he'd borrowed suddenly decided on the due date to give birth to eight offspring, much to the delight of every kid in the neighborhood.

In order to protect the animals, as well as to keep fingers and hands from getting chiseled by sharp teeth, each potential borrower had to attend a special animal handling class, then be tested by museum staff to confirm their knowledge. Before little Ricky was able to check out Petunia the skunk, for example, he had to know that to pick her up he needed to carefully place his hands beneath her back legs and chest, and also that she shouldn't be handled more than three to five times a day, always before feeding rather than after, and never when it was hot. He would have to be aware of her diet, which allowed meat, vegetables, dog biscuits, eggs, and milk. Further, she should be fed only once a day, in the evening. (Giving too much food wasn't really an issue for Petunia, though, since she'd simply stop eating when she'd had the right amount.) Finally, Ricky had to know that the former stinker couldn't be left in the sun for more than ten minutes and should generally be kept in a room with an even temperature, free of drafts.

Beyond all that, Ricky would have to explain where Petunia would live in the wild—a cave? a tree? a burrow in the ground?—as well as what survival tricks she might use. His parents had to sign a release saying they fully understood and accepted the terms of the loan, and also acknowledging they were the ones ultimately responsible for Petunia's welfare. Forbes divided the animals into tiers, depending on the level of care they required. First-division animals—including domestic rabbits, hooded and white rats, white mice, guinea pigs, and turtles—could be loaned out to any qualified child. Second-division animals, which included chipmunks, skunks (deodorized, of course), snakes, and domestic white ducks, were loaned only to kids age ten and older with considerable previous experience. A final tier was established for schoolteachers, Scout leaders, and older teens who'd demonstrated competence in animal handling. In that group were raccoons and porcupines, though the porcupines went out only in locked cages.

Once Petunia returned to the museum, she'd remain there for at least three weeks before being loaned out to another child. Notably, more often than not borrowers at the animal lending library came back with name change suggestions. "The lively little hamsters," reported the *Saturday Evening Post* in 1954, "all come back nicknamed Hammy or Frisky or Butch. All the mice are Mickey or Minnie, and all the ducks are Donald."

For all the grinning, delighted kids and for the dizzy run of national magazine stories and photo ops, John's arrival in California marked the beginning of one of the most hectic periods of his life. As it turned out, though, and much to his good fortune, he wouldn't be walking the path alone.

"We met in Georgia," recalls Margaret Forbes, John's wife of fifty-four years. "I'd been teaching school in North Carolina. But I decided I wanted to do something different with my life." On leaving her position in 1946, she returned home to Georgia, where she found a well-developed Campfire Girls program in Atlanta. It seemed a good fit. At the time, the Atlanta land preserve known as Fernbank (at that time a centerpiece of environmental education in the South) was struggling with deciding what to do with their property—seventy acres of virgin poplar and white and red oak, underlain by a spectacular understory of sourwood, sumac, and dogwood. At an impasse, with the board of directors squabbling, Fernbank decided to send a letter to youth groups across the region, including the Campfire Girls, inviting them to a meeting to help sort it all out. The guest speaker would be John Ripley Forbes—a name being openly celebrated in such circles, thanks in large part to Eleanor Roosevelt's praise of John's Hornaday Foundation in her nationally syndicated newspaper column. On spotting Margaret in the audience, John asked after her, then penned a note to see if she might like to have lunch.

The couple would see each other again during a Campfire meeting in California, and still again in New Hampshire, on Birch Island. As they grew close, it became apparent to John that his vagabond lifestyle, which while earning millions for the cause of children's museums yielded peanuts for him, wasn't particularly well suited to marriage and children. Swallowing hard, he began what he later referred to as "the hardest years of my life," taking a job with a regular paycheck to rekindle the ailing Museum of History and Industry in Portland, Oregon, as well as organizing a new facility in Seattle. The Oregon museum was on thin legs, sporting a tiny office, a scant budget, and a handful of exhibits housed in the lobby of a local hotel. In little time John managed to gather dozens of new displays, secured a $20,000 private home as temporary housing, and quadrupled the budget. His work in the Northwest was aided by a support organization he'd started shortly after leaving the Army, called the National Foundation for Junior Museums. While there's little mention in John's letters of any time off, he managed some on at least one summer day—June 6, 1948—when he summited Mount Hood, thus becoming a proud member of the Mazama Mountain Climbing Club.

For all his success in the Northwest, John was troubled that the museums he was building, or in some cases re-creating, were all designed for adults. He fairly ached for the chaos of wide-eyed kids hovering over exhibits, jumping out of their skin for the chance to touch a live animal.

Then a miracle of sorts occurred. Major Max Fleischmann—the man Forbes had argued with while in the Army, debating the value of live animals in children's museums—passed away, leaving much of his considerable fortune to a philanthropic trust. His widow, Sarah, impressed by John's work, convinced the trustees to offer him a grant of $50,000 a year for five years. Fifteen thousand dollars would go to operating expenses, with the rest to an endowed fund to create additional museums. Overnight, John's prospects exploded. The board of his National Foundation for Junior Museums granted him an annual salary of $8,000 and hired a secretary. They then put on the payroll noted nature artist J. Robert Sewell, hiring him to design backgrounds for the bird and mammal displays needed for the new museums.

With coins in his pocket and a spring in his step, John hurried back to Georgia for the girl he'd fallen in love with, marrying her in Atlanta on December 10, 1951, at the Episcopal Cathedral of St. Phillip. The ceremony complete, they wasted no time heading west again, taking their honeymoon at Timberline Lodge on Mount Hood—a magnificent mountain retreat created as part of Franklin Roosevelt's Works Project Administration. Since the month of December was hardly suitable for another climb of Mount Hood, John chose instead to introduce his bride to skiing, which she immediately fell in love with.

From there the newlyweds headed to Sacramento, where both the city school board and the directors of the California State Fair were eager for John to set up a junior museum, complete with an animal lending library. It was a perfect project, explained the directors, given that the theme of the 1952 California State Fair was "Youth." A building was offered to house the facility, but only on the condition that John got it up and running by the time the gates to the fair swung open in September. Using the Junior League as his front guard, in sixteen weeks John raised $13,000 (equivalent today to about $112,000), designed and constructed more than two dozen exhibits, hired a staff, and rounded up 200 animals for the lending library. Eventually he agreed to serve as director of the California Junior Museum without salary for two years, fine-tuning what was in many ways his signature facility. By the time he left, more than 500,000 visitors, mostly kids from around the state, counted themselves among his biggest fans.

Judging by records—at both the California Junior Museum in Sacramento and the eight California museums that sprang up in its wake—injuries to animals in lending libraries were rare. Nor were there many serious bites or scratches. Still, Forbes was aware of the potential for big problems with poorly run live animal exhibits. Soon after the California Junior Museum opened its doors, his National Foundation for Junior Museums produced a list of guidelines for anyone hoping to launch a live animal program.

1) All animals available for loan are checked by a competent veterinarian, have received their proper shots and are certified as tame and safe to handle.

2) No animal goes into any home unless the museum staff has visited the home and are certain that conditions are satisfactory and that all rules of the Animal Lending Library will be respected.

3) No child may borrow a pet, regardless of their parents' permission, unless the museum staff is sure the child is competent to take complete and proper care of the pet.

4) All animals returned to the live museum after being on loan are checked by the staff or veterinarian before being allowed to again go on loan.

5) A spot check of homes in which an animal is on loan is made periodically and without advance warning, by a member of the museum staff.

Despite occasional newspaper reports to the contrary, children were never allowed to borrow most of the larger animals. Raccoons, native cats, and foxes weren't part of the loan program but were used instead only on the premises, supervised by museum staff.

As for how the animals were actually acquired in the first place, that problem was neatly solved soon after the first newspaper article appeared. Hundreds of parents, suddenly regretting how in a weak moment they'd let Junior purchase a skunk or toad at a nearby pet

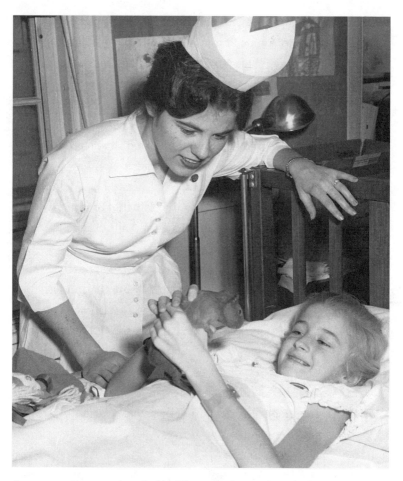

A young patient at a hospital in Westport, Connecticut finds a little comfort from nature, courtesy of the Mid-Fairfield County Museum's animal lending library.

store, were more than happy to contribute to the cause. At the same time came farmers, ranchers, state game rangers, and hunters who had stumbled across abandoned birds or injured rabbits, squirrels, foxes, and raccoons. When the facility in Sacramento first started, nearby State College got into the act, sending over several snakes, a squirrel named Chester, and a female pack rat named Whiskers and her babies—the latter so popular that lending times had to be reduced to just two days.

Although both live museums (where animals never left the grounds) and the new animal lending libraries were growing ever more popular, not everyone was happy about it. Some had concerns about animals switching locations so often, even with three weeks of rest in between. Others felt that having enjoyed the company of a chipmunk or squirrel for a week, a family might be tempted to start wildlife collections of their own—a practice that (much like now) could lead to problems for animal rescue agencies. Meanwhile, a handful of directors strongly objected to the word *museum* being in any way associated with such programs, fearing the term was already being hijacked for roadside collections of the weird and tawdry.

Groups like the American Humane Association were at first cautious, mostly worried about animals being sent out so many times during the year. Well aware of those concerns, John invited the San Francisco Society for the Prevention of Cruelty to Animals (SPCA) to thoroughly review his program. They concluded that while such efforts would in some cases be ill advised, Forbes' approach had the potential to have "beneficently educational results." The biggest development "in the use of live animals to educate children to kindness and understanding," concluded the editors of the *National Humane Review*, "is being made by Junior Museums and Children's Museums of many cities. The movement is being effectively pushed by the National Foundation for Junior Museums."

Forbes continued to speak out—loud and often—against those trying to conduct live animal programs without adequate facilities, training, and supervision. He knew a number of children's museums,

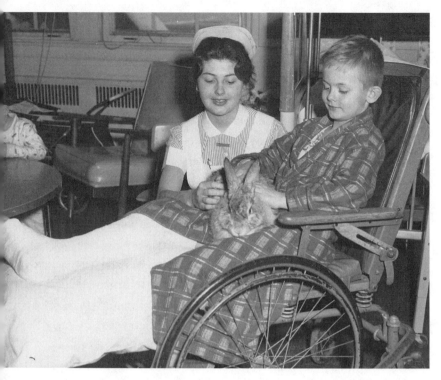

Like most of John's animal lending library programs, the one at Mid-Fairfield County Museum in Westport, Connecticut made a concerted effort to bring animals to sick and injured children in local hospitals, often with the help of local volunteers from the Junior League.

he explained, "which have a few unhappy animals on display in badly designed cages. Such a situation completely destroys the benefits that the Live Animal program can offer. Anyone seeing such abuse should report it to the local humane society and law enforcement authorities and demand action."

He also spent considerable time typing letters to concerned peers. Writing in 1959 to local humane society member William Ziegler of Stamford, Connecticut, who strongly objected to a plan to install an animal lending library at the Mid-Fairfield County Youth Museum (today the Nature Center for Environmental Activities), Forbes devoted two and a half pages to reassurance. He wrote: "I am glad leaders in humane education work like yourself are ever on the alert to protest against programs which may not have the best interest of our animals at heart." He also told Ziegler that he had discussed the effort at length with Mrs. Harry Long of the Humane Society of the United States, as well as with William Kennedy of the Connecticut Humane Society. "I have asked each organization to appoint a member of its professional staff to occupy a position on our Live Museum Committee in order that they can assure themselves and their members that our program is a sound and deserving one, and be in a position to help advise with us, and correct if necessary, any feature which might not be satisfactory."

Though captive animals remained a sensitive topic for years, advocates stood their ground. In late summer of 1965, a person identified only as "Animal Lover" wrote to the *Town Crier* in Westport, Connecticut, to decry the treatment of animals in the nearby Mid-Fairfield County Youth Museum. "My reaction was so mentally upsetting that I returned two days later at an early hour to make sure I had actually seen the things that had kept me awake between visits." These things, said the writer, included inadequate water, messy cages, and myriad animals casting furtive glances, clearly wanting nothing so much as to get out, as well as the opossum and flying squirrel "that want to hide and sleep all day long but have no blessed hole or tree stump to crawl into." "Let's confine education activities," the author concluded, "to stuffed specimens and displays of artificial and natural wildflowers."

The writer might as well have said Westport was hiding communists. Board members and volunteers, Humane Society representatives, and dozens of the museum's regular visitors fired off angry rebuttals, overwhelming the newspaper with letters supporting the facility. "The museum," explained director Patricia Walker, "has been visited by State and Federal Fish and Game officials, as well as museum and zoo directors, all of whom have proclaimed our Live Animal Area outstanding, both as to design and care of the animals."

One of the more interesting responses came from fourteen-year-old volunteer Clare Frances Mills—a member of the museum since age eight—who with her parents' permission seemed eager to set the record straight. She explained that Junior Staff members put in more than 300 hours a week cleaning, feeding, watering, and playing with the animals. She described in detail the cleaning of cages, though admitted that sometimes cages can look a little messy: "We cannot say to the animals 'You must not mess your cages up or some of our visitors may be offended.' Nor can we tell Whipple [the raccoon] he must not play with wood chips in his water dish." Clare continued: "I've never felt that our animals were mistreated or unhappy. If this were true they'd be long dead."

She also refuted Animal Lover's claim that only stuffed animals are appropriate for museums. Asked Clare:

> Have you ever seen blind children feeling one of these animals? Well, I have. Their faces come alive with excitement and they bubble all over. Do you think they would receive this satisfaction from a cold, dead specimen? The faces of the retarded children who visit our museum always take on a serene look after they have held our animals. Can a dead specimen do this? Many an ill child at Norwalk Hospital has found

comfort in a visit from our animals. For a short time each week they are able to forget their pains. Could a dead specimen comfort them in this way? Can you be so cruel as to want to deprive the afflicted, ill, under privileged and privileged child of these things?

Two weeks later, Forbes himself would write a major article for the *Town Crier*, flush with photographs, once again pointing out the special attention given to the museum's live animals and reiterating the glowing reviews given his work by no less than the *National Humane Review*. Animals that grow up and are able to take care of themselves, he explained, are released. Forbes wrote:

> Many of the animals in the Live Museum are brought to us as babies, with their eyes closed. They are brought in by people in the area who find bird nests, squirrels, and rabbits injured by cats or dogs, or whose mothers have been killed. No private home has the facilities to care for these orphans. The local Humane Society does not have the personnel or facilities for this type of operation. So the museum, with its large incubator and dedicated professional staff are able to care for these animals until well enough to be released.

Christian Nelson, chief interpreter for the East Bay Regional Park District in Oakland, seemed barely able to contain himself in a letter of support for the live museum idea. "In all my years of professional experience, I have yet to recall a youngster who started out on a lifetime love affair with nature through an interest in geology, astronomy, botany or the related sciences. Nature's myriad fascinating

John believed in the power of introducing children to live animals, as had his famous mentor, conservationist William Hornaday. Hornaday argued that when it came to teaching kids, what was needed weren't dispassionate lessons, but living, breathing inquiry.

creatures hold center stage, always have, and always will. It is a well-known fact that many movie stars used to have written into their contracts a provision that they would not be required to appear with any animal." Nelson even managed to tie certain social problems to a lack of exposure to animals, claiming that "a youngster who is turned off by the stinging, biting, poisonous, scary beasties of nature because he or she goes on hearsay rather than face to face contact, will grow up being turned off to ecology." He went on to assert that animal lovers are less likely to be bigots or people haters. "If one can learn to love, or at least tolerate and understand all nature's creatures, I am certain he stands a better chance of growing up to love, tolerate, or at least understand his fellow man."

To John, animals weren't just entertaining. They were also a means of opening a child's sense of wonder. Some kids would follow the scent of that wonder with ever-growing sophistication, asking increasingly profound questions, delving deeper into the realms of critical thinking and scientific inquiry. Others found that wonder a spark to creativity— in the playfulness it engendered, in the prompts given to artistic expression. And again, cultivating such qualities seemed more and more important as technology began overtaking more and more of a child's day. To John's way of thinking, no matter how interesting the television show—or thirty years later, how intriguing the computer game—nature in general and animals in particular were powerful teachers for developing our most cherished human qualities.

In January 1950 some 5,000 educators, politicians, and academics came together in Washington, D.C., for a much-discussed event known as the Midcentury White House Conference on Children and Youth. Forbes heard about the conference in the spring of 1949, writing to one of the organizers, Katherine Glover, to wrangle an invitation as a representative of the Hornaday Foundation. By fall there was still no word, so John wrote another letter, this time to his ardent supporter Eleanor Roosevelt. After expressing regret that he wasn't able to connect with Roosevelt some months before in Hyde Park, where he had planned to show her a new film about Hornaday

Foundation activities, he queried whether she could possibly pull some strings to get him into the Children and Youth Conference. "I would greatly appreciate it if you would be willing to suggest to whoever is responsible for the planning of this conference that I be invited to participate and represent the William T. Hornaday Memorial Foundation."

He soon had his invitation.

It was a curious event. Renowned pediatrician Dr. Benjamin Spock talked about the proper role of parents, highlighting the need for "genuine personal affection"—a clear reversal from earlier parenting theories, which among other things advised against hugging children for fear of compromising their independence. True parental love, Spock went on to say, "considers the child not just as its own, but held in trust for the community." Margaret Mead, meanwhile, pointed out that in America "children have had to learn to love parents whose example they could not follow, to listen to the lullabies from the lips of a mother who could not speak the language well enough to order bread and butter from the shopkeeper, to accept at least partial discipline from a father condemned by his inexperience of this new country to work as an unskilled, often exploited laborer." We have given our children an incomparable heritage, said Mead—a willingness to go out into new places among new people, a willingness to stand on their own feet and answer for their own deeds. Yet helping them cross the bridge from the world of their parents, to a world of their own, would require careful guidance by professionals in human behavior.

For his part, President Truman talked about the dilemma of children in a time of war. We cannot insulate young people from the uncertainties of the world in which we live, he explained, nor from the impact of the problems that confront us. Said Truman: "What we can do and must do is to equip them to meet these problems, to do their best to build up those inner resources of character which are the main strength in our democracy."

To John, of course—and for many other educators as well—building character and promoting critical thought were things especially well suited to the out-of-doors. On one hand John was impressed with the conference. But he was also shocked that no one even mentioned the idea of nature having a positive role in child development. The only place the word *nature* was even uttered was in a session on leisure, when Forbes himself brought it up, much to the relief of participants from the American Camping Association. Yet just mentioning it wasn't enough. By the end of that session Forbes had dashed off an official resolution, scribbling on a sheet of Hornaday Foundation stationery: "It is recommended that this conference go on record as encouraging and implementing more and better camping for children and youth. It is further recommended that this conference go on record as favoring and fostering a better understanding of the natural environment resources and conservation among children and youth through proper out-of-door nature trained leadership."

There's no evidence his resolution was ever considered. Acknowledging in a letter to organizer Melvin Glasser, of the Social Security Administration, that no conference could address every need, John remained incredulous at the oversight. "It seems to me utterly unthinkable that any group of assembled youth experts could seriously prepare a platform which would completely ignore the great importance of out-of-doors nature recreation as a character-building factor for youth."

What made the omission all the more striking was that barely a decade earlier, the outdoors had been widely thought of as among the most powerful tools for child rearing. That by 1950 this idea would have so faded as to be ignored by the experts suggests at the very least a sea change in academic thinking. For the next fifteen years John would be swimming against the tide, keeping the value of nature for children alive at a time when the whole country was consumed by promises of a new, highly industrial brand of convenience and entertainment. By the late 1950s even children's museums were pulling away from their traditional underpinnings of nature study—the time-tested framework established by Anna Billings Gallup in Brooklyn as well as by Dale Griffin of Boston and Arthur Carr of Indianapolis. "Each of these pioneer's museums," explained Forbes, "started out with their first collections consisting largely of mounted birds, minerals, shells, etc. The main reason they were set up was to fill a tremendous lack in the community and in the school system, where countless children were left without any real answers to the questions they had [about] the natural history around them."

It wasn't that Forbes was opposed to junior museums having a strong focus on things like history and art. But he was solidly against anyone proposing to bury all traces of nature study. Directors who succeeded the founders of the junior museum movement, he maintained, were by the 1950s rarely being trained as naturalists. Some seemed to have little use for nature at all. What was once a celebrated children's museum in Washington, D.C., Forbes pointed out, had—under the leadership of a woman bereft of any background in natural history—come to focus instead entirely on drama and history. The place quickly failed. "It is obvious that anyone operating a Children's Museum in Washington," wrote John, "would want to have a very big program in history and social science as well as nature. Perhaps more so than in most parts of the country. But the natural history, even in this location, must always be the foundation and basic factor in the setting up of the museum." A comprehensive study of junior museums done in 1956 by Frank Gale of Stanford found most directors still rated "training in science and natural history" as the most important factor for their work. Yet, as far as John could tell, that training wasn't happening. It was one of the big problems he hoped to counter with the programs he was setting up around the country.

"That's what made John a great man," says one of his friends today. "When to most people sharing nature with children wasn't so important any more, he knew it still was."

By 1952 the California Junior Museum was walking on its own, albeit with a few missteps and stumbles, carrying nature's delights to kids and parents and to movers and shakers throughout greater Sacramento. A major membership drive was under way. The Junior League was giving speeches to every imaginable civic group, from the Sacramento City Council to the California State Fair Board. The board of directors convinced popular television personality Ralph Edwards to bring his *Truth or Consequences* show to Sacramento on April 15, with all proceeds going to the museum. By late winter, school groups had booked the facility solid every day until June.

Evening talks were rolling, too. The museum's "Junior Scientists" were busy coordinating a Junior Museum Science Exhibition involving some 1,800 boys and girls from Sacramento and Yolo Counties. "Aroma" the striped skunk had arrived, as well as a friendly gopher snake. The waterfowl pond had nearly a full complement of birds from the Pacific Flyway. The lending library had grown so popular that the directors finally closed it for a week to catch their breath. Soon, letters of inquiry arrived from other museums, from South Dakota to North Carolina. And yet, for all this activity, the program was hardly flush. In the second edition of the museum's newsletter, *Paw Prints*, the editor pleaded for "a supply of ash trays, a few flower vases, a large 40 cup coffee urn, a couple of hot plates, and surplus tools of most any kind."

It's worth noting that as the 1950s wore on—even as leading educators seemed to be losing touch with the value of outdoor education—requests for junior museums grew at a lightning pace. By 1954, in California alone, Forbes had programs under way in San Mateo, Fresno, San Rafael, and San Jose—most of them undertaken at the request of city and county government and school boards. When John was asked to speak, his opening presentation would include a short movie he'd made in Nashville, portraying schoolchildren as well as ailing kids from local hospitals taking great delight in a menagerie of rabbits and chipmunks and skunks. In San Jose, as the end of the movie flickered across the screen, he stood up and offered to kick-start a local program with a $1,000 grant from the National Foundation for Junior Museums, along with $2,000 worth of exhibits. The only condition was that the people of greater San Jose raise the remainder of a $15,000 budget. Six months later, with Forbes as their advisor, San Jose had its own junior museum in Alum Rock Park.

The eventual director of the San Jose Junior Museum, Larry Miotozo, would take cues from stories of John's and Ada Neville's work in Alabama, traveling about to different rural schools with as many animals as he could comfortably fit into his Woody station wagon. Aware that the location of the museum facility in Alum Rock Park wasn't all that convenient for a lot of borrowers, Miotozo also tested the idea of outfitting a trailer as a mobile lending library, which would allow him to pick up and deliver animals to both urban and rural areas throughout the county.

In 1953 *Time* magazine, impressed by John's remarkable success planting museums around the country, did a short feature on him. They were especially taken by his accomplishments in Kansas City, describing how museum officials there "were frankly baffled by the young man with the booming laugh." In the fourteen years that had passed since that project, the reporter went on to say, Forbes had repeated his performance many times, becoming "the Johnny Appleseed" of nature museums: "He has badgered millionaires, begged and borrowed exhibits, set up children's museums from Portland, Ore. to Jacksonville, Fla. Last week, as visitors streamed into his new museum in San Jose, Calif., Forbes could chalk up No. 18." But at age forty, *Time* assured its readers, John Ripley Forbes was far from through: "His present targets: museums in San Mateo, San Rafael, Fresno and Stockton, California, and a $500,000 permanent endowment for the foundation. 'If I were three people.' John said, 'I couldn't get done what I want done.'" Of course the article was read by thousands of people across the country, many of whom decided that their towns too needed a similar dose of magic.

Throughout these years John wasn't simply launching programs, hiring directors, and fleeing the scene. "Here were all these young directors who really didn't have that much experience," recalls John's wife, Margaret. "He needed a way to make sure they were well trained." With that in mind he organized a major annual national training conference that went on for decades. Appropriately, each culminated with the awarding of the annual William T. Hornaday Gold Medal, which over the years would be given to a wide variety of professionals, from Anna Billings Gallup to James Clark to TV personality Marlin Perkins.

Yet there was also something else on John's mind. Across America, nature herself seemed to be reeling, overwhelmed by growing threats from not only pollution but also an explosion of residential and commercial development. By the 1960s there was no mistaking that the nation's open spaces and natural assets were fast disappearing, especially near urban areas. John wanted to do something about this. His work began right back where he'd roamed so many years before—along the shimmering shorelines, in the hushed forests of birch, hemlock, and beech of New Hampshire's Lake Winnipesaukee. ❦

Chapter Seven

TO SERVE AND PROTECT

WITH HIS JUNIOR MUSEUMS IN CALIFORNIA sprouting like poppies, in 1956 John, Margaret, and their three-year-old son, Ripley, born in Sacramento in 1953, returned to Westport, Connecticut. The following year, Margaret gave birth to their second child, a daughter named Anne. Margaret recalls that it was good for John to be back in New England again, surrounded by people who twenty-five years earlier had been devoted fans of his work. Beyond all that, here too was the chance for his own family to know the magic of the oak and hemlock woods, the lakeshores and coastlines, that had so enchanted John as a child.

True to form, no sooner was the car unpacked than John was out tending to potential donors. Among these was a conservation-minded single woman of means from Weston, Connecticut, named Katherine Ordway. "The odd thing," recalls Margaret, "is that Katherine wasn't particularly fond of either children or animals. But she liked John, and she became a big supporter of his work."

Forbes in 1960 with his wife Margaret, along with son Ripley and daughter Anne, feeding the birds in southern Connecticut.

A later odd encounter with Katherine laid bare a quirk of John's he'd managed to keep hidden from the family. "Daddy might have been the least mechanically inclined person on the planet," recalls John's daughter, Anne. "He prided himself on it. He avoided fixing things around the house at all costs." One day, with one of his museum projects in desperate need of cash, he got a welcome call from Katherine Ordway, letting him know she had a check for him. Not wanting to lose any time by having her send it through the mail, he jumped in the car and sped off to Weston.

"He gets to Katherine's house," explains Anne, "and she starts apologizing. 'I'm so sorry you drove all the way over here,' she said, clearly embarrassed. 'My checkbook is in my purse, and I've managed to lock the purse in the bathroom.'"

"No problem," John assured her right away. "We'll just take the door off the hinges." Which he did with great proficiency.

"When we heard the story later," Anne laughs, "suddenly it was clear. He knew how to do those things all along."

Not all the early times in Westport were so lighthearted. Soon after settling in, John was visited by his friend Mattie Matthieson of the National Audubon Society. The Society had been keeping an eye on him, Matthieson said. The group was impressed with what he'd accomplished with the National Foundation for Junior Museums. "I know how much of your time goes into raising money," Mattie told him, explaining that by joining forces with the Audubon Society, he'd be free to do the more essential work of setting up actual museums and programs. It sounded reasonable to John. With the blessing of Audubon president Carl Buchheister, they joined forces.

But John, always the maverick, wasn't particularly good at relinquishing control. He was incensed when the California endowment created by the wife of the late Max Fleischmann was diverted into Audubon Society coffers, leaving him with a modest one-year salary. Nor was he fond of the new name for the effort, "Nature Centers for Young America." Given the structure of the board, though, he didn't have the clout to overrule the decisions. In the end he resigned.

"He was forty-seven years old," recalls Margaret. "Suddenly he was faced with starting over from scratch." Never one to bemoan his fate, he set about restructuring his old organization, changing its name to the Natural Science for Youth Foundation. Within the year he was off and running again—planting dozens more museums, first in the Northeast and Midwest, and later, across the South.

About this same time John got a call from the banker of a wealthy woman in McKinney, Texas, named Bessie Heard. Ms. Heard, in her midseventies and without children, had been making plans for her considerable fortune, hoping ideally to funnel it into a project benefitting kids. As it happened, her banker had heard good things about John Ripley Forbes; after the banker contacted John on Bess's behalf, Bess traveled to Westport, where John and Margaret showed her examples of what she might create in Texas. "We introduced her to the Westport center," says Margaret. "She was captivated by it. From then on things moved very fast. She gave the land, John got a fine director, and the people of McKinney totally embraced it. They supported every idea that John, Bess, and the director came up with."

"John and Bess had a very friendly, loving relationship with each other," recalls Margaret. "She stayed in close touch with us through the years, always sent the children Christmas presents." In 1986 John and Margaret would leave their home in Atlanta (having relocated there in 1971) for a brief trip to McKinney, traveling to help Bess Heard celebrate her 100th birthday. In an interview with a newspaper reporter, John remembered giving very specific advice to her back in 1964. He told her: "Put [your money] in a nature center, and the joy of watching the kids and the animals will make you live to be 100." Well, he told the reporter with a smile, she had done both.

❧

As was the case for so much of his life, the thing that kept John refreshed through good times and bad, whether living in New England or Georgia, were summers spent with the family beside the cool waters of Lake Winnipesaukee. The sunlight on Sandy Beach and the smell of the hemlocks were a powerful tonic—a respite from what continued to be a hectic life on the road. "What I recall about being with John on Birch Island," says former neighbor Karen Hilton, who spent summers there as a young child in the late 1940s, "is that he was so much fun. He'd have pillow fights and tickle fights with us kids. When I was about ten or eleven he'd take us on rides in his Chris Craft boat, and he'd always drive really fast." Karen recalls with special fondness the day John came to visit her family in Vermont. She and her brother had stumbled across a dead flicker on the ground, likely killed when it flew into a nearby window. "John said we should stuff it, then set about showing us how. As it turned out, that was the start of our own little nature museum."

The fondness easterners showed for owning vacation cottages in northern New England grew steadily across the twentieth century. Mixed among the new crop of lakeshore cottages, though, were also dozens of America's oldest and most celebrated organized summer camps. By the 1970s, with development reaching a fever pitch and property values skyrocketing, camp directors were feeling vulnerable. That had been exactly the fate of one of the oldest private boy's camps in the United States—Camp Idlewild, on Lake Winnipesaukee's Cow Island, beloved by people across the region.

Established in 1891, Idlewild had routinely advertised in magazines like *Harper's* in the 1920s, promising parents to give their children "development of character," purity of mind and body, and "a cultivation of good manners."

Yet in 1975 it all came to a end, with the camp falling to development, sending shock waves through the directors of established camps for miles around. Among those directors was John Newton Porter, founder of the marvelous 100-acre Camp Kabeyun on Alton Bay. With his bank account shrinking, Porter was convinced that if something didn't change fast, the camp's stockholders would do exactly as they had at Idlewild, selling their shares to eager real estate developers.

Though living in Atlanta, Forbes was also at this time serving as president of the Audubon Society of New Hampshire. ("A lot of Father's work here really started with New Hampshire Audubon," says John's son, Ripley, pointing out the curious fact of a summer resident ending up as president of the state association.) As far as John was concerned, Kabeyun was just too precious to lose. Energetic as ever, he set about convincing stockholders to do the right thing and donate their shares to preservation. Under his guidance, the Audubon Society eventually acquired 75 percent of the stock, set aside a wildlife sanctuary named in honor of the camp's founder, and then helped John Newton Porter establish an endowment fund to keep the camp running for generations to come. At John's suggestion, part of the endowment held scholarships for poor, inner-city kids in Boston and New York, including special programs for students at the East Harlem School.

Putting on his Natural Science for Youth Foundation hat, John also busied himself working to preserve the deeply forested, sweetly tranquil Ragged Island—at the time owned by musician Wheeler

Beckett. Beckett had long spent his summers in a modest house and music studio tucked into the timber. Now age eighty, he was ready to sell the island for $250,000 and retire to South Africa.

John knew Wheeler was a big fan of kids, having spent decades producing children's concerts and training young conductors. "You've spent your life educating children about music," the sixty-four-year-old Forbes told him, "and I've spent my life educating children about nature. We both love this place. Let's combine our interests, and I promise there will be children's programs here for all time." Forbes' plan was for Beckett to knock $90,000 off his price, selling it to the Natural Science for Youth Foundation for $160,000. For his part, Forbes agreed to create a wildlife preserve on the island in Jane and Beckett Wheeler's name, as well as offer a full plate of summer nature programs for kids.

Within two weeks—with no help from outside legal or financial experts—the two men struck a deal. Forbes would put $20,000 down through his foundation, then raise another $1,000 a month from area residents until the entire sum was paid, or until Beckett's death. John converted Beckett's home into a nature center, filling it in large part with exhibits from Yale University's Peabody Museum, then convinced the Audubon Society of New Hampshire to offer science education programs. Part of the island was designated a loon preserve, with sponsorship from the New Hampshire Loon Fund, while Beckett's music studio became a loon museum. Wheeler Beckett died nine years later, in 1986.

It was actually John's son, Ripley, who had first met Wheeler Beckett while serving as loon warden for New Hampshire Audubon in 1974. It was a casual encounter, because Ragged Island was an attractive site for nesting loons. "That gave him an excuse to talk with Father, and that set him off on this entirely different tangent to save

Ragged Island," remembers Ripley, who says his dad always seemed willing to find funds to help out with projects that caught his fancy. At the same time, John needed to see an end point. Says Ripley: "He had to know that he could either solve on his own whatever issues there were, or else get the project to a point where he could turn it over to a group to carry on."

As if Audubon and the Natural Science for Youth Foundation weren't enough to keep John busy, additional preservation work was channeled through the Lake Winnipesaukee Association, born out of an informal meeting held on the deck of his "Hemlocks" cottage in 1970 to discuss Winnipesaukee's deteriorating water quality. Within a few years, however, it became apparent that development was an even bigger concern. Schemes were being hatched to build bridges to undeveloped islands, and once there, to plant hundreds of condominiums. In 1979 John gathered yet again on his deck on Birch Island a strong group of like-minded people, this time to launch a new organization known as the Lakes Region Conservation Trust.

Of the various good deeds done by Forbes' Lakes Region Conservation Trust, arguably the group's most stunning achievement—offering a remarkable glimpse at hustling John Forbes style—was the saving of 140-acre Stonedam Island, just off the western shore of Lake Winnipesaukee. Of the lake's 274 islands, Stonedam is one of the largest, and has long been a favorite of people throughout the region. In 1981 the island's owners shocked local residents by announcing their intent to sell to a development firm named Stonedam Island Associates. "By the time I got involved," Forbes told writer Diana Tabler in 1988, "a developer had been contracted by the family that owned [the] island, and was already conducting percolation tests." At the same time, they were "negotiating with shore residents to buy more land for construction of a bridge."

So upset were residents, especially nature-friendly members of the nearby Hubbard Beach and Spindle Point civic associations, that they began a widespread boycott of the developer. With the majority of the developer's work firmly tied to local interests, Stonedam Associates soon withdrew from the picture, creating an opening for the Lakes Region Conservation Trust. But the family who owned Stonedam was impatient for a deal. After tense discussions they made what most thought an impossible offer: Forbes' group could buy 80 percent of the island for $650,000. The remaining 20 percent would be held in trust, and at such time that it was sold, the group would have the right of first refusal. There was a catch: Lakes Region Conservation Trust would have to come up with the money in six days. If they failed, the land would go back on the market to be sold to the highest bidder. Even for a seasoned fund-raising warrior like Forbes, $650,000 in six days (today's equivalent of about $2 million) was an outrageous demand, especially considering that the trust had almost nothing in the bank.

John gave it the gas. Right away he headed to Boston to establish a command post at the Logan International Airport Hilton. From there he and his fellow trust members started calling on hundreds of individuals, banks, and conservation groups—virtually anyone who might have money to contribute. In some cases the trustees (Forbes among them) signed personal guarantees for loans of $25,000 or more. Incredibly, at the end of five days the group had secured guarantees of $550,000. An astonishing success, to be sure, yet still $100,000 short of the mark. All but out of tricks, John first rattled the doors of the New Hampshire Charitable Trust, then the Forestry Society. Both turned him down flat. Last on the list was The Nature

Conservancy. They too offered a quick thanks but no thanks.

With only twelve hours remaining, John went back to The Nature Conservancy—this time, though, calling on noted conservationist Dick Pough. An avid birder, Pough was the founding president of The Nature Conservancy as well as a guiding force in preserving New Hampshire's magnificent Hawk Mountain Sanctuary. He was the right man at the right time. Waiting in his hotel room, "pacing amid cups of cold, unsweetened tea and scraps of paper containing the names of bankers and other donors," John finally got the call he'd been waiting for. A $100,000 loan from the New England branch of The Nature Conservancy was on its way. The entire $650,000 was confirmed by BankEast at five fifteen that evening, forty-five minutes before the deadline.

A purchase and sale agreement for the island was signed in the third week of August 1981 aboard the U.S. Mailboat *Sophie C*. There Forbes handed over a $65,000 down payment check to Emery Rice, who was representing the former owners. "I don't think the family ever got over the shock," John said. "Clearly, they never thought we could pull it off." The transfer of title took place on March 10, 1982, nearly a year after the original development plans were announced. "We were not Astors," John said of the small group of advocates who formed the Lakes Region Conservation Trust. "We just showed what a community can do with dedication to conservation, concern for future generations, and good support." Forbes said he never doubted the group would reach their goal, though he admits this was partly because "there simply wasn't time" for doubt.

By June 1982—the first summer the island was under the control of the Lakes Region Conservation Trust—two rangers were busy marking and clearing nature trails, building rustic footbridges, and cleaning up widespread damage to the forest from an infestation of gypsy moth caterpillars. Soon a Junior Scientist program was launched, encouraging research projects by gifted science students selected from area schools. Of course there was still plenty of financial work to be done; the group's plan to pay off their loans in six years meant raising in excess of $1 million.

We are very, very pleased with what we've been able to accomplish this year," wrote John, "thanks to the help and support of so many people. What we need now is unflagging enthusiasm, and a lot of money." Within months of signing the purchase and sale agreement, the group penned an impressive document called "Investment/ Financing Proposal for Stonedam Island," which laid out in fine detail returns and tax savings for big investors. Someone contributing $50,000, for example, not only would have his investment returned over five years, realizing on average a 38 percent return in tax deductions, but at the same time would be providing the group with interest-free financing. Smaller contributions, meanwhile, flowed in by the hundreds. "I am close to broke," wrote a Vermont man in a letter to the trust, "but I heard about Stonedam Island. I hope this $5.00 contribution helps." Dozens of fund-raising parties and special events, from socials to canoe races, were held throughout the area.

"Father devoted an incredible amount of time to Stonedam Island," recalls John's son, Ripley. "I think because he'd never been able to find someone who could do what he did, he did it all. And that meant he had to focus." Ripley thinks his father's original vision was to have a national organization, with people just like him in regional offices, setting up nature centers around the country. "It never worked out that way. You just couldn't pull out the association Rolodex and come up with a guy who'd come in here and raise your money, and at the same time be the inspirational person to sell the program."

With more than 1,400 financial gifts—including two critical donations of $100,000 each—Forbes and his fellow trust members were able to board the MS *Mount Washington* on July 24, 1988, travel to Stonedam Island, and along with 500 jubilant supporters, burn the mortgage. With Stonedam firmly in hand, the Lakes Region Conservation Trust—the tiny group that a decade earlier had gathered on John Ripley Forbes' deck—held deed to more than 400 acres of land for permanent preservation. The trust is still alive and well today, holding title to thousands of acres of New England's finest fortune.

Throughout these furious preservation efforts in New England, John and Margaret were living most of the year in Georgia, having moved back to Margaret's home state in 1971. With John working tirelessly, both his land protection efforts as well as his nature museums flowered across the South in magnificent ways. As it turned out, much of the work would take place in the face of overwhelming development pressures in and around Atlanta, at a time when prices for woodlands and open spaces in or near the city were climbing at a dizzying pace.

John's impulse to save green spaces in and around the city of Atlanta was part of a proud, if by then somewhat distant, tradition. In the two decades before John's birth, literally hundreds of parks had been created in urban centers across the nation, including New York, Boston, Baltimore, Denver, Portland, and Seattle. Beyond the obvious opportunities open space afforded for fresh air and exercise, a number of nineteenth-century writers, going all the way back to Alexis de Tocqueville, saw such places as a critical mixing zone for children from disparate economic backgrounds. Cities tended to be places of social extremes, said de Tocqueville—the one thing democracy could never tolerate. In much the same way that wilderness in the 1700s was sometimes called "the great equalizer," a century later similar notions were being applied to smaller, more urban pockets of the outdoors. If wilderness had symbolized to many "an even playing field," with its blessings and challenges available to everyone, city parks would be celebrated as places for rich and poor children alike to come together through outdoor play. This is one reason why, even in the midst of the Great Depression, the federal government continued to earmark large sums of money to keep America's city parks afloat.

One of John's earliest projects in the region was the Outdoor Activity Center, touted in the 1970s as Atlanta's "first and only environmental education and outdoor recreation facility." Just one of twenty-six projects the Natural Science for Youth Foundation was supporting throughout the Southeast, the center was in part an attempt to provide teachers of inner-city youth a chance to bring traditional science classes into an outdoor classroom. As early planning documents describe the project, the staff would be dedicated to "helping make children aware of their surroundings—what living things mean to them and what they mean to their environment." The property itself—eight acres that eventually grew to almost twenty— was leased to the center by the Atlanta Public Schools for a dollar a year. It consisted of an especially beautiful slice of southern forest off Richland Road in southwest Atlanta, a mere three and a half miles from city hall, thick with old-growth maple, oak, poplar, and pine.

Forbes' own description of the effort turned on ideas that would soon become cornerstones of the 1970s environmental education movement. The point of urban preserves, he said, was "to stimulate awareness and understanding among people of all ages, of the complex relationship between man, his cities, and nature." By offering an immersion in fresh air, wildlife, solitude, and educational programs, the Outdoor Activity Center would "impress upon the visitor the necessity of safeguarding nature in an urban environment." The center's first director, Robert Geraci, concurred: "We are challenging the premise that nature and the outdoor experience exists only in the country. How can we expect the child deprived of experiencing the wonders of nature to appreciate that the things essential to his survival come from nature?" In earlier times, Geraci acknowledged, it didn't seem to matter that we lacked ecological insight and understanding. But, he warned, "now this lack threatens the very structure from which we lead our lives."

In a practice he'd followed since the early years of his career, from the very start John tied the fate of the Outdoor Activity Center to local individuals, groups, and institutions. School superintendent Dr. Alonzo A. Crim was courted at every step. Mayor Maynard Jackson was thrilled to hear about the project, assuring Forbes in a letter dated January 29, 1976, that "many civic leaders share my enthusiasm for this location, feeling that the children and adults of the inner city have long needed such a program." Hope Moore, the commissioner of parks, libraries, and cultural and international affairs, confided that while "dreams and ideas as exciting as the center many times fail . . . from what I have seen so far, I know that success awaits us."

Likewise, the board of trustees was set up to include both blacks and whites ("the bi-racial flavor is good for our city," as banker Henry Bowden put it), containing members of the Georgia Conservancy, the Audubon Society, the Botanical Society, and the League of Women Voters. John LaRowe of the Atlanta Planning Department was enlisted as the center's first president. And of course, there was the ever dependable Junior League. Before long, inner-city schoolkids were making regular field trips to the Outdoor

Activity Center, where they were greeted by professional naturalists eager to show them how science, art, and history were firmly linked to their larger surroundings.

When the school board agreed to furnish two small classroom buildings but couldn't afford to move or maintain them, the Natural Science for Youth Foundation stepped in to take on all associated costs until community fund-raising was in place. Beyond its work with school groups, the center was open free of charge to the public, providing rare opportunities for inner-city families to hike and camp. It also offered programs on city ecology and creative arts, as well as nature day camps, evening presentations, and classes in everything from orienteering to horticulture. "It is amazing what can happen," observed *Atlanta Constitution* columnist Bob Harrell, "when concerned people go beyond concern and act."

Eventually, the Atlanta Bureau of Parks and Recreation purchased from the school district the property where the Outdoor Activity Center stood, creating the first link in what would become a dynamic urban forest parks program. The bureau was charged with maintaining the land itself, while the various activities that took place were sustained by grants and memberships. In December of that year, Robert Geraci of the New York City Parks and Recreation Department was hired as director, receiving a salary of $12,000 a year, as well as free rent and utilities at a refurbished home on the grounds of the preserve.

Geraci had strong feelings about not allowing the facility to be called a nature center. "It's an outdoor activity center," he said. "We will be talking about how the concrete world relates to the green world and how both are needed. We'll learn how a city street affects us the same as a tree. The only way we can accomplish this is to make it relevant to the people." He talked often about his experiences in New York City, where several programs took "super poor [kids] from a ghetto like Harlem to the countryside for two hours. The kids saw trees, breathed fresh air and then returned to the ghetto even more unhappy with their environment. Each area of a city should have its own natural areas to enjoy." Through Geraci's leadership the Outdoor Activity Center stayed on the cutting edge, setting an example of how environmental educators could move past the old, entrenched notion (not uncommon even today) that somehow humans are apart from, rather than a part of, the natural world.

In 2007 the National Wildlife Federation referred to the Outdoor Activity Center property as "an ecological jewel." It now includes a natural science museum, complete with a 700-gallon tank built to resemble a freshwater Georgia pond, stocked with catfish, perch, crappie, bluegill, and gar. Hundreds of schoolchildren still roam the three and a half miles of trail in the preserve, which is maintained with volunteer support. A line from the original fund-raising proposal for the Outdoor Activity Center remains a perfect touchstone: "Planned and direct encounters with soil, water, woods and rocks, sunlight and wildlife, under the guiding hand of a teacher-naturalist, is learning that cannot be surpassed."

As the Atlanta Outdoor Activity Center was growing—and at times struggling for survival amid harsh economic times—Forbes and his foundation were also busy helping create the beautiful Chattahoochee Nature Center, on the other side of Atlanta, as well as preserves in nearby Roswell, Toccoa, and Morrow. Chattahoochee especially is magnificent—a riverside weave of pine and oak and cattail and honeysuckle. And like the Outdoor Activity Center, it was founded at a time when few people in Atlanta even knew what a nature center was. "It was embarrassing," Forbes told a writer for the *Atlanta Constitution* in 1986. "A lot of professionals were pouring into the city, and they demanded such amenities for their families. Look at Minneapolis–St. Paul. [They] have twenty nature centers and two major natural history museums." Indeed, in the thirty years that John and Margaret were gone from Georgia, little had happened in the way of making nature more available to children.

Yale graduate Frank McCamey was one of the supporters who fed and watered Chattahoochee—advising on everything from trails to programs, and later serving on its board of directors. McCamey had first become aware of John's work through the *Saturday Evening Post* article about animal lending libraries. Curiously, on that particular topic the two men disagreed. "Both of us knew kids like to have a warm furry critter to touch," Frank recalled when he was ninety. "But John was inclined to use a wild animal, while I voted for domestic ones, saying that children wouldn't know the difference." McCamey explained how John would happily use for his demonstrations a recovered sparrow hawk, maybe one that had been injured by a car; Frank, on the other hand, was happy to have a pigeon. Remembered Frank: "John also believed in trying to save anything that came along—so long as it was still moving and breathing. I'd vote for putting them to sleep, get them out of the picture. An injured animal doesn't always act normally, and that can create wrong impressions about wildlife."

McCamey was among hundreds of old-school, hands-on naturalists who came to work at the junior museums and nature centers John was planting across the nation. As a Boy Scout himself in Memphis, he found a Scout leader who was also an avid bird watcher—a fellow who spent most of his free time pursuing the ranges of southern birds like herons, eagles, and perhaps most notably, the chimney swift. "More than a million swifts were passing over our heads every fall," says McCamey, "and nobody knew where they were going. Well, we found out."

Frank's Scout leader worked for the Tennessee Inspection Bureau ensuring that commercial buildings were in compliance with fire codes and other structural regulations. That gave him unfettered access to tall buildings. "We'd climb up on these buildings at night and put big nets over the chimneys after the birds had gone in. Then in the morning we'd band as many as we could." Franks said that eventually a missionary in the mountains of southern Chile saw natives making gadgets out of the aluminum leg bands and reported it to the States. "Out of thirteen bands of swifts reported to Washington, five of them were our birds from Memphis." (McCamey delighted in telling the story of how birds often showed up in the southeastern United States wearing bands from the biological survey with the words "Wash. Biol. Serv." Said McCamey: "We'd hear about someone crossing paths with a biologist doing field work. They'd complain about how they followed exactly the directions on the aluminum band—washed, boiled and then served—but that the darned things still tasted lousy.")

Despite their philosophical differences, McCamey remained to the end a great admirer of John's work. "I've come a long way since I was doing nature programs for different camps in the Northeast, driving up and down the coast of New England with a horned owl, a couple of turtles, and a bag full of snakes in the back seat." He was grateful to John for taking a chance with him. "Maybe he had to," Frank laughed, still amazed by the force of John's personality. "There wasn't anyone else who'd take a chance with *him*!"

Driving both men was the realization that as children's lives were becoming ever busier, driven ever more by technology, they were losing all experience of the natural world. Both Forbes' and McCamey's efforts were fueled by the knowledge that some of the problems kids faced could be averted by giving them even small doses of nature. Both men understood that in the blink of an eye, a child's sense of wonder could still catch fire.

Each year more than 30,000 people visit the Chattahoochee Nature Center, as well as thousands of schoolkids on field trips. Appropriately, given John's special fondness for animals, in early 2008 Chattahoochee opened a state-of-the-art wildlife rescue and treatment center. The city of Roswell is expanding their river greenway project to include lands fronting the nature center, the idea being to connect to similar trails in Cobb and Gwinnett Counties, forming the metro Atlanta component of the 180-mile statewide Chattahoochee River Greenway corridor. One of the organizations John started in the early days of the center—first known as the Chattahoochee Foundation and now called the Southeast Land Preservation Trust— has raised millions of dollars to save forested areas in metro Atlanta.

"John was tenacious and he was fearless," notes Ann Bergstrom, executive director of the Chattahoochee Nature Center. "I don't believe he saw obstacles where other people saw them. I've heard of people whose feathers he ruffled over the years. But that's the mark of a mover and a shaker. You never accomplish anything if you're just out to appease."

As if land preservation emergencies in New England and multiple outdoor center projects in the South weren't enough, John's Natural Science for Youth Foundation was in this same time period sparking a new project in a handful of the poorest neighborhoods in New York City. Working through the Boys Club of New York with funds from the Heckscher Foundation for Children, the mission was once again to give poor kids the chance to build deeper relationships with their immediate surroundings.

Near Harlem, at the Jefferson Park Center—in 1973 one of three Boys Clubs in the city—John's program director Sally Middlebrooks was serving up a full plate of activities. Boys learned photography, made marine life observation trips to Jamaica Bay, explored ponds on Staten Island at High Rock Park, and took field trips by bus to the American Museum of Natural History, the Bronx Zoo, Central Park, and Bear Mountain State Park. At the American Museum of Natural History, museum staff created special programs for the kids related to the natural history of Africa and Puerto Rico. Every other week in summer, a group traveled to Camp Harriman in the Catskills, where they went on frog hunts, dug up and ate Indian cucumbers, chewed birch bark, discovered what it felt like to lie down on hair cap moss, sprinkled gold dust on their arms from spore capsules, picked blackberries and blueberries and raspberries, and made everything from plaster casts of wildlife tracks to leaf print postcards.

Like John, Middlebrooks was committed to helping the boys forge a stronger sense of place. That meant paying greater attention to what was going on around them. One of Sally's programs, for example, investigated local food, allowing the boys to explore their neighborhoods by finding out what the people living there liked to eat. Considering the rich variety of ethnic groups in this part of New York, they had access to an amazing array of specialty grocery stores. By conducting in-depth interviews with the shopkeepers, the boys learned about basic ingredients favored by different cultures, many of which they'd never heard of. They then went on to study the origins of the ingredients, the history of their use, and when appropriate, their relationship to native plants of the northeastern United States.

In 1970 Sally and John launched a special mobile natural science center, carrying display cases, lab equipment, and even live animals into some of the city's poorest African American and Puerto Rican neighborhoods. The mobile unit also served a request from the Human Resources Center in Albertson, Long Island, where naturalists worked with a group of handicapped children. Austin McCormick, professor of criminology at the University of California, was one of several researchers who had a chance to witness the wheeled lab in action. He said later: "It was one of the most innovative and heart-warming programs that I have ever seen. And one of the most effective for the prevention of delinquency." McCormick went on to say that in his fifty years working in crime prevention, he'd found that one of the most effective approaches was "to provide wholesome, interesting, and if possible, educative activities for boys and girls who live in urban areas"—settings that too often seemed to "exert a downward drag from earliest childhood."

The mobile unit was a great convenience. As Sally Middlebrooks explained in 2007, it was no comfortable business to board the subways with a six-foot-long black snake stuffed inside a pillowcase. Still, the task of carting lab equipment and display cases from center to center in the mobile science center, let alone finding secure parking places, was more than a little daunting. Happily, the Boys Club at Jefferson Park was so pleased with the science lessons Sally offered that they decided to provide space for such classes at their club. The effort soon grew to include a reading area, magnifying glasses and other simple equipment, and of course, a small number of live animals. To make sure the animals were cared for properly, some of the older boys were trained as Sally's assistants.

Middlebrooks, who attended at various times Duke, Columbia, and the Bank Street College of Education on Manhattan's West Side, recalled more than thirty years later that she was eager to take on the work John had helped arrange. "It's troubling," she said, "that kids today are so rarely allowed to simply play outdoors." She would become a passionate advocate for "world building," which refers to children building forts, digging holes, and performing all sorts of other creative acts that occur during unfettered play. "It sounds odd," Sally recalled, "but when we did programs for sixth graders in the north part of Central Park, one of the greatest things that happened was that they simply got a chance to roll down a hill, maybe jump off a rock. Certainly, there's a lot to share with children in nature as far as learning. But unless you catch their imagination, most of them aren't going to connect with what's right in front of them."

Back in the 1970s, as Sally Middlebrooks was roaming the city with members of the Boys and Girls Clubs, John received a letter of congratulations from a distant admirer. "I am pleased to reflect on your years of leadership in enriching the lives of children everywhere," wrote First Lady Ladybird Johnson. "I know of your several projects in my home state—specifically the Fort Worth Museum of Science and History, Corpus Christi Museum, Heard Natural Science Museum and Wildlife Sanctuary in McKinney, and the Austin Natural Science Center. . . . I applaud [your] fine record and congratulate you."

And still, John Ripley Forbes wasn't close to being done. ✎

Chapter Eight

POT PATCH TO PARK

A WARM GEORGIA MORNING, late in June 1990. Drug Enforcement Administration agent Ted Golden hangs in the skies west of Atlanta, his small plane tracing circles above one of the most beautiful slices of forest in southern Cobb County—a land of oak and beech and waist-high azalea, of sweet-tasting springs, of delicate waterfalls tumbling into gardens of fern and moss. But Ted Golden hasn't come to enjoy the scenery. Acting on a tip, he scans the woodlands around four-acre Lake Careco until at last he finds it: a cluster of several dozen waist-high, weedy-looking plants, each showing the telltale green of marijuana.

On July 16 the owner of the property—a mild-mannered forty-nine-year-old named Clarke Poole—is found guilty of violating the Controlled Substances Act and is sentenced to five years in federal prison. After a year struggling against the verdict, his appeals exhausted, Poole becomes increasingly troubled by something beyond his pending jail time. Under a federal law passed earlier in the decade, personal assets related to drug charges, be they money, automobiles, or property, can be sold to the highest bidder, the lion's share of the revenue going to whatever local and regional law enforcement agencies were involved in the arrest. Poole is heartsick to think his beautiful forest will likely be sold and soon afterward be overrun with developers. Imagining those open, unencumbered runs of woodland, creek, and meadow cut and parceled for houses or factories seems somehow a fate worse than his own.

"I called The Nature Conservancy first," he recalls, "to see if there was anything they could do. But the parcel was smaller than what they typically get involved with." Then someone happened to mention seventy-seven-year-old John Ripley Forbes. With time running out, Clarke paid a visit to John at his home. Much to Clarke's surprise, Forbes agreed to investigate. Heading out in August with trusted colleague Charlie Cochrane by his side, Forbes was stunned by the sheer beauty of the place. "I took a look," he later told a reporter, "and I was amazed that something like this still existed so near downtown Atlanta." If one could dream up a place to educate children about nature—wild and untrammeled yet close to all those city kids who needed it most—it would be hard to do better than this. John went on to say that while he never understood why Poole would do "such a fool thing" as growing marijuana on the place, Clarke had five years to figure that out. He knew Poole cared deeply about Careco. Now Forbes was about to show a little fondness of his own.

Within forty-eight hours of setting foot on the shore of Lake Careco, John was making phone calls and writing letters to Congressman Buddy Darden, Governor Zell Miller (Forbes was at the time serving on a Governor's Advisory Committee), Attorney General William Barr, and The Nature Conservancy. "This property is one of the most significant natural areas in our entire greater Atlanta area and must not be sold," he wrote in a matter-of-fact letter to the attorney general on September 17, 1991, submitting his comments as president of the Southeast Land Preservation Trust. Instead, John wrote, it should "be preserved for the benefit and enjoyment of the citizens of the state of Georgia." In the event it wasn't possible to simply transfer this property from federal ownership, Forbes added, "we ask that the Justice Department limit its sale to the State or County at as reasonable of a price as possible." Poole, meanwhile, who by now had started serving his prison sentence, corresponded with Forbes every week, doing what he could to help coordinate a major letter-writing campaign to save Careco.

Long accustomed to running into outrageous obstacles in pursuit of his work, this time John met a brick wall. Placing a phone call to the Department of Justice on August 22, he got a chilly reception. Under present statutes, he was told, the government could retain the land for use by a federal agency for law enforcement purposes (unlikely in this case), sell the land and share the proceeds with participating state and local agencies that helped in the seizure, or sell it and deposit the money directly into the Assets Forfeiture Fund. The Justice Department was set on the second option, which by then had become a prized means of funding law enforcement. Forbes was told in no uncertain terms that Lake Careco would soon be on the auction block.

Undaunted, John kept turning the crank on the publicity machine—efforts that, among other things, lead to an article in the *Atlanta Constitution* on October 12 called "From Pot Patch to Park." After praising both the place and the effort to save it, reporter Charles Seabrook explained that the Justice Department "has thrown cold water" on the conservation effort. He wrote: "Federal law allows the agency to transfer property seized in drug crimes only to other federal or state law enforcement agencies, under the philosophy that ill-gotten gains of the drug trade should become the assets of law enforcement authorities to stem the flow of illicit drugs."

~

The way John figured it, if current federal law was the problem, then he'd have to change federal law. The day after his fruitless conversation with the Justice Department, he phoned the office of Congressman Henry Waxman of California, then chairman of the House Subcommittee on Health and the Environment. Waxman's subcommittee was one of only two in the House of Representatives with jurisdiction over the Controlled Substances Act. John hatched a rough plan with his son, Ripley, who was working as an aide to Waxman. Next, they started hashing out a possible initiative to amend the Controlled Substances Act, working with Georgia governor Zell Miller and prominent members of the Georgia congressional delegation.

The basic idea behind their revision was that the U.S. attorney general would be required to transfer seized property to the state— so long as a request for such action was made by the chief executive of that state—and, most importantly, that the land would be used for recreation, historical purposes, or the preservation of natural conditions. With the auction date for Careco growing close, Georgia senators Sam Nunn and Wyche Fowler made a special request of the Justice Department, asking them to delay the sale. Two days later, after several additional conversations with Forbes, Governor Miller wrote Attorney General William Barr, requesting the property be deeded to Cobb County for the establishment of a nature preserve.

As federal legislation goes, the amendment Forbes and his cohorts were pushing traveled at near light speed. On October 8,

John fought hard while in his 70's and 80's to save some of the last, best remnants of woodland for the children of greater Atlanta. Here Georgia Governor Zell Miller, one of John's allies in the fight for Lake Careco, presents him with the 1991 Conservationist of the Year award, sponsored by the Georgia Wildlife Federation.

Representatives Roy Rowland and Buddy Darden introduced HR 3524, known as the "Controlled Substances and Forfeited Property Amendments of 1991." Immediately after being introduced, the legislation was referred jointly to the Subcommittee on Health and the Environment and the Subcommittee on Crime, within the Committee on the Judiciary.

As it turned out, the Violent Crime Prevention Act of 1991—a separate piece of legislation—was at the time already winding its way through various legislative procedures. Sensing the wisdom of jumping on a boat that had already cleared the harbor, on October 10 Representative Darden, along with Henry Waxman, appeared before the House Rules Committee to encourage the Rowland-Darden provision be added as an amendment to that existing piece of legislation. Unfortunately, though, the House and Senate deadlocked over the 1991 Crime Bill. That, in turn, brought to a grinding halt the Rowland-Darden amendment that John and his colleagues had been working on. If a resolution didn't occur before Congress adjourned—and that looked increasingly unlikely—the Justice Department was almost sure to put the Lake Careco property on the auction block.

Regrouping with amazing speed, within the week Forbes' team turned their attention instead to Senate Bill 1891, introduced by Strom Thurmond of South Carolina on October 29, which dealt with the ability to waive the recovery of federal construction funds used to build community mental health centers in the 1970s. When word came down that Thurmond's bill had passed, Waxman moved fast, negotiating with Senator Thurman—then ranking minority member of the Senate Judiciary Committee—as well as members of the Energy and Commerce and House Judiciary Committee, pushing to add their Rowland-Darden amendment onto the bill. While Waxman wasted no time in these efforts, he also moved very quietly, trying not to attract the attention of the Drug Enforcement Administration, which remained unenthused about the proposal.

In a remarkable display of bipartisanship, within the month the Senate had agreed to add the amendment, clearing the legislation for the president's signature. On December 17, President George H. W. Bush signed Senate Bill 1891 into law, though not without attaching a signing statement meant to help the Justice Department. "It is my intent," Bush wrote, "that transfers of property under section 2 will be limited to situations in which the transfer will not breach the obligations of the United States to any State or local law enforcement agencies entitled by law to a share of the proceeds from the sale of such property." The original language contained in the Senate bill assured states they'd be responsible for only nominal costs associated with seizure, such as paying off existing liens (on the Careco property, these amounted to about $90,000). But Bush's signing statement weakened that congressional intent. By the time Forbes along with representatives from the Cobb County Parks, Recreation and Cultural Affairs Department, the Natural Science for Youth Foundation, and the Trust for Public Land gathered at Careco in the first week of December, taking a moment to celebrate what was by any measure an astonishing legislative victory, trouble was already brewing.

Leaning hard on Bush's signing statement, the Justice Department put a price tag of $359,000 on the property, claiming a need to funnel funds into the coffers of local law enforcement. The price left Cobb County commissioners backing away from the entire deal. Didi Nelson of the U.S. Attorney's office in Atlanta defended the Justice Department's decision to play hardball, claiming the various law enforcement agencies needed their cut of the pie, which would "be used to benefit their citizens." What she didn't say, however, was that four of the nine law enforcement agencies involved in the bust had already waived their $28,000 share of the proceeds for the good of the preservation cause. Finally, after a series of black eyes in the press, Justice suddenly announced that it was planning to turn the property over to the Georgia Sheriff's Association for a youth drug education camp. "This is our way of preserving the land," explained Didi Nelson.

In the fall of 1992 noted congressman John Lewis, whose district had swelled to include some of southern Cobb County, paid a visit to Careco. In a masterful stroke of publicity, he brought with him students from Bryant Elementary School, many of whom had written heartfelt letters in favor of the nature center idea. The entire bunch strolled through the trees under the wary gaze of federal marshals.

At long last, in October 1992—more than two years after Ted Golden looked down from that small plane and spotted Clarke Poole's marijuana patch—there appeared an opening in the standoff. The idea was to open Lake Careco to children throughout the nine months that school was in session. During summer months it would be reserved for a combination environmental–drug education program, under the management of local law enforcement agencies. An announcement finally came on October 15, courtesy of Attorney General William Barr at the Atlanta Hilton. Though the feds would still be turning Careco over to the Georgia Sheriff's Association—instead of to Cobb County, as was originally hoped—it would mostly be used for what John Forbes was fighting for all along: a natural science center, learning laboratory, and summer camp for school-age children. "We want to turn the kids on to nature and off of drugs," explained Bob Carter, associate executive director of the Georgia Sheriff's Youth Homes.

For the first time in history—under a federal law little known even today—property seized for criminal activity was being transferred for educational and recreational purposes. "It took a lot of players," recalls John's son, Ripley, all moving against a Drug Enforcement Administration that he describes as greatly vexed. "Father was the one who made it all work," says Ripley. "And much of it was done on a handshake. You could never assume that [John Forbes] was just the ornithologist, the expert on nature. He knew how to play politics."

Just as both Clarke Poole and John Forbes knew would happen, all around Careco, in every direction, development has surged—a tidal wave of warehouses, offices, and small manufacturing facilities. Yet in Careco the big mountain laurel continues to bloom. Waterfalls still whisper across moss-laden rocks. In springtime kids wander among magnificent clusters of native azaleas, which in this place show a curious range of colors found almost nowhere else: white, yellow, orange, red, and pink. And all these years later, Poole, who until recently was working at a teen treatment center in North Carolina, feels incredibly grateful. "John was a savior," he says. "I'd always seen that piece of land as sacred, and suddenly I was losing it because of my own mistakes. John showed up and gave hope."

If John was a master of the nature preserve down the street, he also still delighted in thoughts of far-flung places. In January 1989, at seventy-five years old, he was invited to serve as naturalist and guest lecturer aboard the 435-foot Argentine supply ship *Bahia Paraiso*, ferrying eighty passengers to the icy waters of Antarctica. Having sailed as a young man to the Arctic with Donald MacMillan, he was thrilled by the idea of roaming untrammeled sweeps of the southern polar regions.

Early on, the journey seemed particularly blessed, the travelers moving south on a sun-drenched morning in January out of Ushuaia, Argentina. Even the Drake Passage—infamous for its howling storms and fierce water—was utterly calm, surprising even veteran explorer and cruise leader Peter Bruchhausen.

The ship made an initial call at the permanent Argentinean base of Jubany, home to about 16,000 penguins and more than 500 sea lions. From there they worked their way to several other international bases, delivering supplies at each stop, then on to the stark volcanic terrain of Deception Island. At the end of the tour, the passengers embarked on a fine overland foray in full sunshine at America's Palmer Scientific Station. Here too there was an abundance of wildlife, from south polar and brown skua birds to Wilson's storm petrels, Weddell and elephant seals, and an Adelie penguin colony containing between 9,000 and 12,000 pairs of breeding birds. By late morning the passengers were back on board the ship with hugely contented grins on their faces. Soon afterward began the first of three lunch shifts. A little after two o'clock the *Bahia Paraiso* weighed anchor and fired up her engines, sailing out of Arthur Harbor, homeward bound for Argentina. Having finished his meal, John headed to his cabin to get his camera, hoping to capture some final shots of the shimmering white mountains in the distance, and the cold, steely water, the drifting ice flows.

"Suddenly," he later wrote in his journal, "without warning there was a terrific jolt, a loud crash as the ship's bottom hit a ledge. I found myself flying across the cabin, falling upon the bed as the ship came to an abrupt halt, leaning aft and to starboard." Meanwhile, those who were just sitting down to eat in the mess hall tried to hold on amid crashing plates of food and flying bottles. "As I picked myself up," wrote John, "I heard one panicked sailor yell 'we hit a whale!,' but it was soon obvious we'd hit a solid ledge." The engine was shifted into reverse and revved to top speed, then quickly cut as the engine room flooded with seawater. Related John: "As the ship continued to list, a shaky voice in Spanish over the loud speaker said we must prepare to immediately abandon ship."

Leaving everything behind and donning life jackets, the

passengers assembled for evacuation with admirable calm. The crew feared that unloading the motorized lifeboats with the mechanical crane could capsize the ship, so instead passengers were lowered into fifteen rubber life rafts, which were then to be towed to shore by outboard-powered launches. Nerves flared when one of the motors on the launches wouldn't work; worse still, it soon became obvious that the crew had no idea how to row. In the end the rescue was completed by a fleet of Zodiac rafts, courtesy of a Society Expeditions cruise ship anchored nearby, which towed the launches the mile and a half to Palmer Station.

It was astonishing that John Ripley Forbes would yet again find himself run aground in some far, frozen corner of the world, fifty-two years after the *Gertrude Thebaud* was high centered in Frobisher Bay. But while he and the other passengers were rescued quickly from the sinking *Bahia Paraiso*, hardly worse for the wear, the land itself—those delicate, wildlife-rich coastal zones—fared much worse. This time John and his fellow passengers suffered more than just another shipwreck. It was also the first major ecological disaster on the Antarctic continent.

Incredibly, the crew of the ship not only had been warned of the dangers of this ocean but had survived three close calls on the inbound trip. Indeed, after the ship had first anchored, the liaison officer at Palmer Station advised the captain that the approach channel he'd used was extremely dangerous and that on departure he should avoid the route at all costs. Yet on setting sail again, the ship not only turned into the same risky passageway but did so at high speed, somewhere between eleven and fourteen knots—nearly three times what would have been prudent under such conditions. The ship crashed at the exact point on the navigational charts where the warning phrase "rocks and pinnacles" is written. The impact of the collision ripped a thirty-foot-long gash in the side of the vessel, releasing 170,000 gallons of diesel oil.

"I would say it's going to be a very, very serious thing—a major oil spill," Forbes told National Public Radio shortly after the event, while on his way back to Georgia. "The krill, which is the key food of the wildlife, is going to be eliminated. And once those penguins hit the water, that's it. It's a tragic situation."

Dead krill washed ashore almost immediately. Adelie penguins, dripping oil, made their way to nesting sites on Torgersen Island; soon their chicks fledged, 40,000 of them heading off into a sea fouled with petroleum. Seals grew sick, and some died. The intertidal zone was severely damaged. To make matters worse, in the days following the disaster the weather turned brutal, delaying for over a week the arrival of equipment needed to contain the spill. Some observers shared a hope that the ship, still perched atop the rocks, would break up and sink before spring. So too was there talk of dynamiting her, cutting her up and carrying the pieces out to sea. The spill remained big news, covered by media around the world. At least it was big news until March 24, when coverage evaporated in the face of yet another ocean disaster, this one off the coast of Alaska, involving the *Exxon Valdez*.

Troubled by the potential devastation of one of the most fragile ecosystems on the planet, 75 year-old Forbes returned home to Atlanta determined to do something about it. Awestruck by the beauty of the region, he declared himself "a convert," eager to support a prohibition against energy development in Antarctica. "The wreck of the *Bahia Paraiso* is a warning to all who love this last great continent. It must be kept in its unspoiled state," he urged. From Atlanta he called friend Roger Tory Peterson, asking advice about setting up a protective organization for the region. Peterson,

John Ripley Forbes, standing in the last of a long string of urban nature preserves he helped create. This one, known as Big Trees, is located on the outskirts of Atlanta in the city of Sandy Springs.

in turn, directed him to celebrated international conservationist Sir Peter Scott (founder of the World Wildlife Fund), who was at that very time working furiously to have the Antarctic established as the world's first international park. After talking with Scott on the phone, Forbes wrote him a letter, obviously excited. The letter read in part: "If I were to help in any way with your ambitious dream of seeing Antarctica become an International Park, this could be the biggest land preservation project ever attempted. Many will say it's impossible, but unless some of us make the effort, Antarctica may well be lost and the world will suffer great environmental damage."

Despite the fact that there were by then already well-organized scientific organizations speaking on behalf of the Antarctic, Forbes continued to mull over the idea of a more citizen-based advocacy group, one that could also serve as a coordinating tool for existing conservation efforts. Those who had already visited the Antarctic, he speculated—be they tourist, scientist, or support personnel— could be among the charter members, pledging to pressure their respective governments to preserve the region, including supporting Scott's plan for an international park. Working mostly with Peter Bruchhausen, over the next year the duo envisioned the details of such an organization. "We could start this with about $20,000 for the first year," Peter told John early in 1990. "I would need $1,500 per month, plus $2,000 for office supplies, mailings, printing, phone calls etc. Do you think we can raise the above amount in the next 60 days?"

In the end, though, Bruchhausen's furious schedule—not to mention John's, which was about to heat up with preservation efforts in north Atlanta—along with strong movement by similar groups forming in different parts of the world, kept the organization from lifting off the ground. John nonetheless remained a strong advocate for the region, writing articles for various newspapers and journals, talking with great urgency about the precious Antarctic to anyone who cared to listen. ❧

Chapter Nine

THE FINAL FOREST

THE LAST BATTLE JOHN FOUGHT, as poignant as any, was for a small but thoroughly remarkable tract of old growth forest at the northern edge of Atlanta, in the city of Sandy Springs. Lying just east of traffic-laden Roswell Road, tucked between a police complex and a new car dealership, the area known as Big Trees had all the marks of a classic Forbes rescue: a precious slice of nearly forsaken nature with developers ready to fire up the bulldozers, and enough political intrigue and massive fund-raising demands to leave even seasoned conservationists trembling with fear.

By the time the struggle for Big Trees started brewing in the summer of 1989, Atlanta was losing tree cover at the rate of fifty acres a day. In the following half dozen years, the city's urban footprint would expand a whopping 47 percent, while Georgia as a whole would see more than a million acres of farm and forest fall to development. In short, it was the kind of boom that made acquiring undeveloped property, especially prime acreage, extremely important and, at the same time, terribly expensive. Some argued that spending so much money on such small acreage was crazy—that one could get a bigger bang for the buck up north, where land was cheaper. "But that's not where the people were," explains John's wife, Margaret. "That's not where the kids were."

As in most of the rest of America, by the 1990s kids in Sandy Springs were having an increasingly hard time connecting with nature. Rampant development was only a part of the problem. The era saw a profound erosion of America's relationship to the outdoors, with the amount of time kids spent doing anything outdoors declining drastically. What play there was seemed to increasingly reflect adult obsessions with staying busy, filling the days with things sure to produce either obvious comfort or obvious improvement. Young children were being so saturated with brain-building tools that psychologists felt compelled to issue a warning to parents, reminding them of the importance of unstructured play. In roughly the first decade of life, the therapists pointed out, a child's brain development turns less on intellectual processing than on sensory stimulation. Rather than offer a barrage of gadgets to promote mind-based learning, kids were said to get more of what their brains actually needed by climbing a tree or playing in a creek.

A creek, for instance, like the Powers Branch, which flows like a slow waltz under the hushed canopies of Big Trees. When writer Nora Waln declared that the woods give peace to the souls of men, surely she was thinking of a place like this: a mix of massive red and white oaks, some measuring more than forty-five inches across; hickory and holly, sassafras and sumac, red maple and redbud and wild cherry. Not to mention some of the most beautiful beech trees for hundreds of miles. Beneath these grand sweeps of leaves in many months are explosions of wildflowers, from Solomon's seal to bloodroot, from

Located in the city of Sandy Springs, "Big Trees" had all the marks of a classic Forbes rescue: a precious slice of nearly forsaken nature with developers ready to fire up the bulldozers, and enough political intrigue and massive fundraising demands to leave even seasoned conservationists trembling with fear. By the time the struggle for Big Trees started brewing in the summer of 1989, Atlanta was losing tree cover to development at the rate of fifty acres a day.

violets to trumpet vines to rare native orchids. In these woods, said biologist Frank McCamey "is a sample of that primeval forest of 300 years ago. In fifty years of forestry and botanical work, I have never seen more exceptional specimens."

That such a rich refuge existed in the feverish bustle of a growing city is even today something visitors find astonishing. "I take my kids here in the afternoon, right after I get off work" says one nearby resident. "There are days we arrive anxious, out of sorts. When we leave, though, the world seems fresh again."

Because of the exceptional quality of this woodland—in particular, the fact that it holds the kind of elderly white oak and beech trees all but gone from the region—the stand had been fairly well known among local conservation groups. Still, in the summer of 1989 the Fulton County Planning Commission voted unanimously to rezone seventeen acres of the old growth along Roswell Road, giving a green light for development by the Grove Corporation. Not long afterward an amateur naturalist riding by on his bicycle saw a "for sale" sign among the trees and sounded the alarm. But in fact the sale was already being negotiated—part of a plan calling for virtually all the trees to be cut down to make room for a pair of car dealerships. On July 14 a consortium of representatives from Trees Atlanta, Sandy Springs Clean and Beautiful, Sandy Springs Historic Community Foundation, and Sandy Springs Citizens—led by John Forbes' Southeast Land Preservation Trust—requested a meeting with the Grove Corporation, presenting a plan to protect seven acres of the tract for a permanent nature center. To their credit, Grove agreed to defer the zoning variance hearing, accepting a sixty-day moratorium on any development to allow a feasibility study for the preserve.

At the time Big Trees went up for sale John had several other balls in the air, including helping coordinate a $3 million center at Cochran Mill Nature Center and Arboretum, as well as working with the county to secure a long-term lease on sixty acres of magnificent laurel and azalea woodlands at a place called Autrey Mill. Arguably, at seventy-six he was well past the age when most men set about slaying dragons. Yet given the feverish pace at which nature was being lost in urban Atlanta, he was adamant that exceptional open spaces like Big Trees be protected for kids.

In September 1989 he requested another meeting with executives of the Grove Corporation, where he was granted an extension of the development moratorium until October 1. Working tirelessly, ten days before the extension expired he managed to negotiate a plan acceptable to Grove. With a $100,000 down payment due in ten days, to be provided by Southeast Land Preservation Trust, John would purchase seven acres for $2.9 million—$600,000 less than the original asking price. John further convinced Grove not only to donate an additional three acres at no cost, raising the preserve to ten acres, but to cover engineering and architectural services relative to the planning and building of a nature center. "They were very cooperative," Forbes told a reporter for the *Atlanta Constitution*. Then, flashing a smile, he confessed to having resorted to some rather punchy tactics, planting in the minds of company executives images of "little old ladies chained to trees and children standing in front of bulldozers."

The funding scheme was tangled at best. Success depended heavily on the Fulton County commissioners, who were to come up with the lion's share of the price. But the county had a long list of priorities considered more important than a nature preserve on Roswell Road. Forbes pressed on, writing a letter to the commissioners on September 27, laying out the vision. He wrote: "I plan to raise from area foundations $1,000,000 to be used toward the purchase of the property. We need a firm action by the county that they will pay the balance of $1,950,000 over a three year period, starting with their 1990 budget." John further explained during the commissioners' regular meeting of October 5 that he would stand up and make this offer in public, as well as declare a pledge that the ten acres would be handed over to the county, so long as there was a lease for those working on the long-term maintenance of the preserve. "The land will become a nature park, complete with a nature center for the enjoyment, use and learning of school children of Greater Atlanta. When the property is fenced along Roswell Road for the safety of the children, we're sure it won't be long before this preserve in Sandy Springs becomes recognized as being as beautiful as DeKalb County's Fernbank Forest."

In a meeting presided over by Lee Roach, fellow commissioner Tom Lowe proposed that the plan be supported in principle. That motion was seconded by Commissioner Hightower and supported by Roach and the only other commissioner present, Martin Luther King III. The conservationists were off and running.

Of course there remained the not inconsequential task of raising $1 million. John immediately wrote grant requests of more than $500,000 to various foundations, along with a plea for an additional $100,000 from the state of Georgia. Fourteen local citizens with deep pockets were sold on the notion of adopting individual trees—six of the oldest and biggest went for $10,000 each—raising roughly another $100,000. Finally, being in Atlanta, it made sense for John to approach the Turner Foundation, which had a history of being friendly to issues concerning nature and the environment. But try as he might, he was having no luck getting a meeting. Finally John made a call to fellow Georgian Jimmy Carter (Forbes had campaigned for Carter in 1976). The former president wrote a note to Ted Turner right away, encouraging him to meet with Forbes.

When John reached the end of his allotted fifteen-minute appointment, Ted Turner asked him to stay a bit longer and tell him more about the project. In the end John walked away with $50,000.

"Mr. Turner explained to John that [when it came to getting the money] his foundation only met quarterly," recalls Big Trees board member Randy Pollard. "In the interim, John asked me to see if my Uncle, Dr. Jordan Callaway, of Covington, would make a partial three month loan until the Turner Foundation grant came in. John knew Dr. Callaway was a lifelong conservationist, living on a thirty-acre wooded property not unlike Big Trees." Pollard admits to being a little nervous asking his uncle for that kind of help, but in the end the doctor agreed to at least hear more about the effort. Recalls Pollard: "In a short phone call John convinced him to make the loan—and to my amazement, got him to do it a second time when the first three months ran out."

Like other Forbes projects, not every supporter of the Big Trees Preserve had deep pockets. From the very beginning Big Trees had cast a spell on schoolteachers, local garden and horticultural club members, hikers, and nature lovers of all shapes and sizes. Within weeks of the project getting off the ground, children were dumping coins into large fund-raising buckets located at ten area schools, each school aiming for $1,000.

Despite a growing tide of public enthusiasm, under the full body of the Fulton County Commission there would begin some rather spectacular foot dragging, in the end nearly sinking the effort. And in the face of such delays, the Grove Development Corporation was getting anxious. "The challenge, John," Grove vice president Dick Olson wrote to Forbes on December 14, 1989, "as we have known for quite a while, is timing." Olson went on to say that his company had commitments they "absolutely cannot extend without seriously jeopardizing our overall development project." A week later, Fulton County Commission chairman Michael Lomax—once on the board of the Outdoor Activity Center—deferred action on Big Trees, claiming he was "not going to be blackmailed by anybody into making an inappropriate decision."

Seven months later, with bulldozers ready to start knocking down trees, the county still hadn't given final approval. Then, on May 16, 1990, immediately prior to the commissioners' voting on whether or not to use the county's bank credit line to finance the preserve, the *Atlanta Constitution* ran a feature editorial encouraging the politicians to do the right thing. The editorial read in part: "Critics will be tempted to say that by borrowing money in order to establish a nature park, the commission shows it cares more about trees than about people. That would be a false accusation. The question is whether it is worth using extraordinary means to preserve the Big Trees Forest. If commissioners take the long view and consider the value of this beautiful bit of nature to present and future residents of Fulton County, they will conclude that it is well worth it."

In the end they did just that, with the effort being led by Commissioner Tom Lowe. "The miracle seems to have happened," Forbes told a reporter. One day before John's seventy-seventh birthday, on August 24, 1990, the ten-acre Big Trees Preserve was deeded to Fulton County. "John made it happen," said one supporter of the project. "And he did it in a way that made everybody win."

As always, standing by John's side through all the stress that came with saving Big Trees was his wife, Margaret. "I think I was the thing that held him down on the ground, where reality was," she says today of their years together. "We were alike in lots of ways, in that we both loved the outdoors. But I'm more cautious than he is." She recalls the day, in the middle of the fight for Big Trees, when John told her he had just co-signed a note for $1 million. "I said, 'John, you're always putting yourself out on a limb.' The next day we drove to New Hampshire for a vacation, and all the while time was ticking on the 10 percent interest note. I told him, 'Whatever you do, don't you dare get hit by a truck.'" Clearly, here was a man who embodied that old favorite saying of the optimist: take the leap, and somehow the net will appear. "The difference with John," says Margaret, "is that he *made* the net appear."

Four years later, at age eighty-one, John Ripley Forbes was at it again, this time appearing before the Fulton County Commission in May 1994 to convince them to pay for half of the $1.2 million needed to expand Big Trees by another ten acres. The commission deadlocked on the proposal. Days later, though, Fulton County land agent Diana Hunt approached John, suggesting the county might be willing to purchase the tract with funds already set aside for land acquisition, so long as a corner of the property could be used for a planned senior citizens center. On June 1, 1994, the county approved that idea by a 5–0 vote. (The county would later decide on another site for the center, leaving the entire ten acres for Big Trees.)

Even then Forbes wasn't quite finished. The following year, on his eighty-second birthday, his Southeast Land Preservation Trust obtained a 100-year lease from the state of Georgia for ten additional acres for Big Trees, at a cost of $600,000, bringing the size of the preserve to thirty acres.

John had great success in his ventures in large part because he created conditions where passionate, competent people could see a clear place for their talents. In the work to preserve Big Trees, one of those people was Charlie Cochrane—a gentle man with a profound reverence for nature, who had built or cared for countless miles of trails in parks, private lands, and national forests throughout the region.

Cochrane would become the face on the ground at Big Trees,

embodying the vision of John Ripley Forbes in a daily practice of the woods. He organized trail crews and helped build bridges, hauled shredded bark, slashed away at privet, and watered trees during drought. Those who came across Cochrane in the woods were immediately drawn to him, pulled into his orbit by the kind of calm, patient strength that emanates from people doing exactly what they want to do. In addition to working with hundreds of Scouts and schoolchildren, Cochrane forged connections with forestry students in Georgia, creating opportunities for graduate students to earn research credit at Big Trees. "I've never been so happy as when I was on my knees in the dirt, working next to Charlie," recalls an Eagle Scout who worked at the preserve in the late 1990s. "There was something about him that made you want to reach deep and do your best. I always figured that 'something' came out of the woods."

Margaret recalls the afternoon in 1989 when there was an unexpected knock at the door and she and John opened it to find Charlie Cochrane standing there—a man neither she nor John had at the time ever met or even heard of. "But he knew about John," Margaret recalls. "He so wanted to meet him that he just came over unannounced. In his hands he had all these pictures of the places he loved." Margaret says the two men fell fast into friendship. "They were like two peas in a pod—all but finishing each other's sentences. They were that close in what they were dreaming about." This was about the time John first learned about the threat to Big Trees; soon Charlie was going out with him on negotiations, then on trips to scour funds. "All of his life Charlie had been searching for something," says Margaret. "First he was in a rock band. He went to law school. Then he got into refrigeration work. But when he met John, it was like he suddenly found his life."

In the summer of 2007, just a year after John's death at ninety-three, Charlie died of a heart attack. Fittingly, his last breath would come under the arms of the great woods of Big Trees.

〰

The old adage "nothing breeds success like success" is no less true for preservation than for business. On hearing about the victory at Big Trees, other landowners approached Forbes to find out whether their property might be appropriate for preservation. At the same time, people with increasingly diverse skills and backgrounds began moving onto the preserve's board of directors. One man in that mix—at first glance, a most unlikely champion—was well-known Atlanta developer Charlie Roberts.

"When John was trying to save Big Trees," Roberts recalls, "the property actually belonged to a neighbor and friend of mine, a developer named Charles Sheron. He was the guy planning to build a car lot there. Out of nowhere comes this tree hugger, John Forbes, and he starts trying to stop the project, mess up my friend's deal. Back then especially, any time you had a great piece of land worth a lot of money, and a guy shows up and starts talking about trees, it wasn't exactly a welcome thing."

Curiously, when John finally got Big Trees under contract, leaving his group to raise $1 million of the purchase price, he approached Roberts for a contribution. "Think of the most inspiring minister you know, preaching about God, and that's the way John felt about Big Trees. He just didn't want to take no for an answer," Roberts remembers. Roberts thought about it but in the end decided to pass. "I figured he'd get it done one way or another. And in truth, at the time I didn't much value that sort of thing."

As the years passed, Roberts sometimes found himself walking the trails of Big Trees, where he usually ran across that passionate steward of the preserve, Charlie Cochrane. Part of what kept him coming back, though, was his young daughter, born in 1987. "She gets to about five years old and all of a sudden I'm wondering, hey, where's the park? Where do you take kids around here?" Roberts says he sometimes tells people that if they want to educate others about the value of something, they need to see the value of it in their own lives, from their own perspective. In the end, the combination of years of unfettered, unbalanced growth in greater Atlanta along with a desire to give his daughter time in the forest left Roberts with a fresh perspective. "All of a sudden I saw a greater good—one that a younger man or woman might not see. I began to really appreciate what John had done. I began to appreciate Big Trees."

About this same time, on one of his development projects in Gwinnett County, Roberts had the notion of putting twenty acres into a conservation easement, hoping to give it stronger protection than what could be gained from a simple homeowner's agreement. He spoke about it with Charlie Cochrane, who not surprisingly was hugely enthused about the idea, at one point inviting Roberts and members of the Gwinnett County Land Trust over for a tour of Big Trees. "So we show up," recalls Roberts, "and there in the mud and the dirt, on his knees, was Charlie Cochrane, working on the creek bed with ten or fifteen volunteers. I couldn't believe the boss, the director, was down there in the mud. Soon enough I came to understand that this is where he always was." Cochrane, showing the kind of enthusiasm that moves mountains, started explaining to Roberts the ties he'd established between Big Trees and the Boy Scouts—in particular, Eagle Scouts—who'd done phenomenal work building trails and designing and constructing bridges at the preserve. "I decided that's what we should do in Gwinnett County," Roberts explains. No doubt sensing the gifts a man like Roberts could bring to Big Trees, Cochrane suggested he join the board of directors. Roberts recalls: "I said no, I'm probably not the one to do that. And I left."

But Big Trees wouldn't leave Roberts alone. He kept seeing the value of the place. He felt the board could benefit from the kind of help his years of experience as a businessman could provide. "It's all about timing," he says. "About where you happen to be in your life. As John's health declined, his usual iron hand and strong leadership, which had made everything work, just wasn't there anymore. Charlie Cochrane was totally dedicated to being in the forest, being with people, being a teacher. And he was the greatest teacher you could ever hope to see. But you can't be the teacher, the trail builder, do all the maintenance, and at the same time pay the bills and raise the money."

Roberts's move to the Big Trees board of directors happened quickly, just months before John's death in late summer of 2006. Weak and frail, one day John got dressed and he and Margaret drove to Roberts's office. There, along with board member Charlie Cochrane, Forbes began sussing out Roberts to see if he was a good fit. "It was a very moving experience," recalls Roberts. "Seeing this very fragile ninety-three-year-old man, obviously in the last few months of his life, but with such integrity. This worker, who even at that meeting was all about accomplishing things—a guy who you knew had suited up and played the game every single day of his life." Roberts thinks part of what impressed John during their initial meeting was Roberts's office building—a remarkably graceful structure, which he'd managed to slip into the forest with an amazing degree of sensitivity to the surrounding woodlands. "Maybe he figured that if I'd go to that much trouble to save the forest around an office building, then surely I understood the need for Big Trees."

Margaret, who of course knew John's vision better than anyone, was there to help out during that meeting, asking her frail husband questions, pulling directives from him for the rest of the group. "John gave me my marching orders," recalls Roberts. "Margaret seconded them, and Charlie was the third. The next thing I know I'm president of the board of directors for Big Trees. I made a commitment to John and Margaret and Charlie that day. I became a part of saving this place."

In many ways Big Trees seems a perfect last chapter in John Ripley Forbes' long and lovely body of work—an effort that involved government workers, private citizens, corporations, schoolchildren, teachers, journalists, developers, and bankers. After all, saving the last slices of nature that they might continue to inspire Americans for generations to come was to John always an act of community. And if he's no longer here to convince us of the need for such action, then perhaps we can rise to the occasion on our own, inspired by his extraordinary success.

Big Trees continues to be cared for by volunteers from throughout Atlanta. As invasive plants like privet are removed from the forest, local master gardeners fill in the spaces with native shrubs and flowers. Thanks to Charlie Cochrane's earlier leadership, the Boy Scouts continue to play a major role in the preserve. In August 2005, on the occasion of John's ninety-second birthday, Boy Scout Michael Black wrote a letter to Forbes, thanking him "for all the work you have done for our world over the years." At the time of his letter, Black was working toward a conservation medal known as the William T. Hornaday Award. "I am very interested in Mr. Hornaday," he said, "as I believe that he, not unlike yourself, sets a great example of what we as stewards of our Earth should strive to do in order to maintain it." Black concluded by telling John how much his work means to someone of his own younger generation: "Thank you for helping to save a piece of forest in our city, and thank you for everything else you have done. Mr. Hornaday would have been proud."

The hard work of preservation goes on. Perhaps among fans of Big Trees, though, it goes on with a little more pluck and spirit than in some places, what with their having witnessed the miracle of what can happen when people join together for a common good. That John Ripley Forbes' energy and political savvy will be missed in future efforts goes without saying. Yet of all the splendid notions he passed along in his lifetime, one of the greatest is the wisdom to carry on in the face of discouragement and skepticism, when resolve begins to flag. His skills aside, John kept winning in large part because he kept believing.

By any standard, his legacy is astonishing: more than two dozen preserves totaling over 2,500 acres. In greater Atlanta alone he was a major player in establishing the Outdoor Activity Center, the Chattahoochee Nature Center, the Reynolds Nature Preserve, the Cochran Mill Nature Center and Arboretum, the Autry Mill Nature Preserve and Heritage Center, the Dunwoody Nature Center, the Preservation Oaks Sanctuary, and the Sandy Creek Nature Center in Athens. In 1946 he worked with the Board of Fernbank to establish the Fernbank Children's Museum—later run by the Dekalb County schools, becoming the celebrated Fernbank Science Center.

He was the founder of fifty-four museums and natural science centers in forty-one states and was the go-to guy for another 150 communities struggling to establish nature centers of their own. He served as director of seven different children's museums, from Kansas City to Nashville to Sacramento. He was a Conservationist of the Year and a Nature Educator of the Year, and he was given recognition and achievement awards by everyone from the U.S. Forest Service to Who's Who. Big Trees is now officially known as the John Ripley Forbes Big Trees Forest Preserve.

"He never seemed to care much about getting credit," says John's son, Ripley. "It didn't matter who got to stand up and be handed a plaque and have their picture taken. It was the getting it done that mattered. It was always about saving more outdoor space for children to learn about the natural world." ❧

Epilogue

IN ADDITION TO ALL THE INSPIRATION held in the nation's last wild places—be it the great runs of hardwood forest in Great Smoky Mountains National Park, or the wind-blasted peaks of Glacier and Yosemite—Americans will continue to forge much of their views about nature from the things that sprout nearest their front doors. What John sensed happening back in the 1950s, as television claimed more of the time children once spent playing outdoors, has swelled to crisis proportions. Research in 2006 by Oliver Pergams and Patricia Zaradic suggests that "videophilia"—a rising cultural obsession with virtual media—is causing an even more dramatic shift away from the direct experience of nature. Another study predicts that today's fourteen-year-old, by the time she reaches age seventy-six, will have been plugged into phones, computers, televisions, and other electronic devices for a mind-boggling total of twenty-eight years. True, television and the Internet can expose us to aspects of the outdoors, especially the science of a place, in new and refreshing ways. But they're no substitute for the essential experience of nature, for encounters that recast the imagination and that allow us the strength of heart needed to save the very world that sustains us.

As of this writing the United States is losing more than 6,000 acres of open space every day. Current estimates suggest that by 2025 the nation's population will increase by more than 60 million people, resulting in the need for an additional 30 million new homes. As John wondered aloud back in 1995, at age eight-two, while surveying the explosion of apartments along north Atlanta's Peachtree-Dunwoody Road: "Where are the children going to play?" If some in Atlanta were shocked at the price paid for the initial ten acres of Big Trees, in the not-too-distant future such prices may well seem like a bargain.

Preserving our relationship with nature on many days requires the sort of grit and pluck so often displayed in the saving of Big Trees. And Stonedam Island. And Chattahoochee. It takes local politicians embracing the idea that good leadership means helping people make not just a living but a life. Within such acts of courage— preserving a tract of urban forest here, a creek or a meadow there— lies sufficient spark to light the hearts and minds of Americans for generations to come.

It's one thing to admire a man like John Ripley Forbes for the strength and steadiness of his trajectory, for the kind of vision that allows some people to see flowers long before the season of their bloom. But beyond that, John never lost touch with that precious sense of wonder that nature presents to anyone who cares to embrace it. To his own children, and to countless others, he was a playful, hearty source of both marvel and knowledge, turning walks in the woods into entrancing adventures. For a man always reaching beyond mere names or theories of things, perhaps the outdoors was special to John in the way it was to those sitting in rowboats off Birch Island in Lake Winnipesaukee back in 1897, bringing the sun down on a Sunday evening with rounds of hymns. Beyond the preacher's words, beyond any doctrine, was the simple, unwavering urge to turn their faces to the dimming sky and begin to sing.

Photo Credits